# SURRENDER
## (BUT DON'T GIVE YOURSELF AWAY)

SPIKE GILLESPIE

# SURRENDER
## (BUT DON'T GIVE YOURSELF AWAY)

OLD CARS,

FOUND HOPE,

AND OTHER

CHEAP TRICKS

 UNIVERSITY OF TEXAS PRESS, AUSTIN

Printed in the United States of America

First edition, 2003

Requests for permission to reproduce material from this work
should be sent to Permissions, University of Texas Press,
P.O. Box 7819, Austin, TX 78713-7819.

⊚ The paper used in this book meets the minimum require-
ments of ANSI/NISO Z39.48-1992 (R1997) (Permanence of
Paper).

LIBRARY OF CONGRESS CATALOGING-IN-PUBLICATION DATA

Gillespie, Spike.
  Surrender (but don't give yourself away) : old cars, found
hope, and other cheap tricks / by Spike Gillespie.
     p.    cm.
  ISBN 0-292-72850-6 (cl. : alk. paper)

  I. Title.
  PN4874.G386   A25   2003
  814'.6—dc21                                           2003010208

This book is dedicated to

    Claudia Kolker

and

    Michael Stravato

and

    Nancy Brzuska

for years of ongoing faith

and hope and encouragement.

**And,**

    as always,

to

    Henry Mowgli Gillespie,

my Love,

for his unconditional everything

and his extraordinary patience.

**We're all allright.**

"Surrender," *Cheap Trick at Budokan*

# CONTENTS

## ACKNOWLEDGMENTS

I have been blessed with more friends than anyone else I know. People generous with their time, patience, food, money, encouragement, faith, hope, and love. I can't imagine how Henry and I would've made it this far, this well, without these friendships. Listing everyone would require a separate book. Still, I would like to thank the following folks (and pray all y'all whose names do not appear will forgive me that).

Special thanks to Theresa May and Allison Faust and the University of Texas Press for seeing my idea as viable and making it happen. To Meredith Phelan for helping me get the earliest draft together. And to Kate Messer and Mary Carter, who edited so many of the original versions of these pieces. To all the publications who agreed to run these essays in the first place, including: The *Austin Chronicle*, the *Austin American-Statesman*, the *Washington Post, Bust, Gargoyle, Salon.com*, Austinmama.com, and *Thecommonspace.org*.

Thanks, too, to Ross, Jonny Vee, Michael Fay and the Rev. W. Blake Gray (for all the early pointers), Jill, Kenan, Kat, Everett, Hank Stuever, Sarah Barnes, Tom, Vadym, Steph, Amy, Paul, Diane, Makoto and Kiyomi and Junko Sadahiro, Michael McCarthy, John the Baptist Talbird, Bob Vivian, Paula, Olivia, Kristie, Wendy, Melanie and William, Mister Hayashi, Molly Ivins (for all the advice and, better, the stories), Lisa Kresl, Hector Cantu, Mary Kirk, Elizabeth Royte, Dan Hardick, Sue Neal, Anna Lombardo, the Lasser-Foster ensemble, Deanna, Mitch and Melissa, Jeff Krebs, Ann and Hilary and Nick and Will and Sophie and Stella, Sarah and Phil and Emma and Eli and Pip and Scooby and Alison, Sue and Megan and Doris, Jeremy and Bookpeople, Marty Berger, Dean Robinson, Kim Lane, Chris McDougall, Ken Martin, Eric Van Danen, Pam LeBlanc, Robin

Bradford, Ruth and Brad and Neil Heaney, Penny Cipolone, Leslie Tingle, The Pogue-Freeman Menagerie, Riki Dunn, Todd Rhoades, Steve and Erin, Jeff Tietz, and Steve Van Wicklen (who, it is important to note, is not the dentist referred to in the "Pain Hurts" essay). To Janet Boyle for the concrete support. To everyone who read thebelljar.net and contributed to the cause. To everyone in my family who makes our Jersey trips so fun. To all my wonderful readers in Dallas—with special thanks to those who took the time to send kind words of hope and support. To all of you who read my online "column" (word slop fun), with special thanks to those of you who've been reading since '95. To Teresa Wingfield for a great cover. And to Satch, Tatum, and Bubbles for being the best officemates I could hope for.

## SURRENDER
### (BUT DON'T GIVE YOURSELF AWAY)

I've been writing since I figured out how. That was over thirty years ago.

Through words I have learned to surrender without giving myself away. I put it all down—the painful, the funny, the mundane, the embarrassing. I share it through publication and am humbled and moved—to tears of pain, gratitude, disbelief, joy, and deep resonance—when, here it comes, whipping back at me. No matter how personal, unpleasant, or peculiar an experience I describe, I'm always greeted with empathy in return.

The letters come in: *That happened to me, too,* they say, going on to console and validate me, to shock and soothe me. The circuit completes. Reminding me how very unalone am I.

And so, here, a collection of some of those pieces that have given me release and brought me comfort (in the writing, in the responses). There are odes to my good days and bad, to trips I've taken—both real and metaphorical, to holiness found in unexpected places, to men I have not slept with, to learning to live sober. Too, there are miscellaneous ruminations on my alter-ego, my inner-teen, the floor mat in my car, a dead squirrel in the road.

I first met one of my best friends, Jonny Vee, when we were teen waiters at the Jersey Shore. Years later, Jonny once introduced me to another friend as having been, back in the day, about the angriest person he'd ever met. That assessment surprised me at the time, and I flinched.

Still many more years would have to pass before I could look back and see where that observation had come from. I was a so-called "over"-sensitive child in a home with a hard-ass dad in a small blue-collar town with little patience for creative and academic dreams—precisely the dreams that filled my head.

In that town, in that childhood, in that house, I found plenty of hope despite some pretty negative circumstances. But then there were moments when hope would be dashed, seemingly gone for good. Or so I thought, until, oddly, hope again appeared. It was a relentless cycle, a sort of he-loves-me-he-loves-me-not exercise where, as in a surreal dream, the flower petals never run out.

I have hope. I have hope not. I have hope. I have hope not.

But of course, when you have hope—once you have learned it or been given it or recognize its existence within you (hope springs eternal, okay, sure, but from where?)—hope is the dominant force. The real petal plucking then, goes more like this:

I have hope. I have no patience, so it feels like no hope. Oh, but wait, I do have hope, here it comes creeping up on me again. No, hang on, there it goes again. Oh, wait, here it comes again.

Hope. What a bizarre, gorgeous oddity.

I have a grandmother who is past ninety. She has had far more moments of hope-dashed than I. She was orphaned at a very young age and sent to a violently abusive home. She was separated from her siblings. She married in her teens and had seven children with an angry man. One of them died. She raised the other six kids through the Depression. She waited on tables so many years, when other women didn't work—they stayed at home.

My grandmother, Murphy Mom-Mom, still has hope, still sparkles, doesn't look a day over seventy. Perhaps it is in having her in my life that I have not feared getting older. In fact, I love getting older. Now on the cusp of forty, my body is slower but my vision just keeps getting clearer. With age comes perspective. So I sound like a cliché? At least it's a happy one.

I look now, and I see clearly a ridiculous abundance in my life, an abundance the young and angry me was not so quick to recognize. Or, really, that the young and angry me simply could not recognize, not without going out into the world and inadvertently learning to diffuse anger in all sorts of ways, collecting, haphazardly, a stunning number of eye-opening experiences.

This collection reflects that stumbling abundance. It is a tribute to the hope and faith that have somehow stayed with me through some pretty damn dark times. It is a big fat thank you card to all the experiences that brought me to the realization that my life is exactly how I want it to be, and an even bigger thank you that I have been able to recognize the fullness, now, as it is occurring in every moment.

I can't thank you enough for taking the time to read my words.

# DRIVING FORCES

# BREAKING UP

It was time. I knew. I was sad. But resigned, too.

Our last weeks together, sentimental thoughts of four years filled me. All we'd been through, the places we'd traveled, how smooth the ride had (mostly) been.

Then older memories came, ghosts of other conclusions reluctant. I missed them all, even the ones that suffered breakdowns, left me stranded.

You see, I'm one of *those* people. Lover of crappy old cars.

Counting vehicles I've bought, half-owned with boyfriends, or been given, the total is eleven. Cumulatively, I've spent $4,750. Average cost per car: $431.81.

Not bad.

This is my father's legacy. The man purchased only fixer-uppers, often exercising street poet's license in defining said task. Like the old convertible bought from the guy across the street. Ragtop ripped, Daddy built a square, aluminum siding roof for it, slapped a coat of aqua house paint on. I don't think the neighbor ever forgave him.

My first car, a '64 Valiant, was the Flintstone mobile. Holes for floorboard. Chicken wire securing exterior wounds. A hundred and fifty bucks. We were both seventeen. First love. Still miss it.

Late '82 I scored a '67 Dodge Dart Swinger to carry me to the nearby state college. I transferred out of state, leaving it behind. Lived car-free 'til '85 when a good chunk of student loan procured a '63 Galaxy 500, ample chrome shinier than a new toaster, performance far less reliable than same.

Next came tandem purchase with evil college boyfriend—a '67 VW camper to follow some illusionary hippie bliss. But he was a whiner scared of the open road and his controlling ways did not approach the groovy kind of love required for our lofty goal.

I left him, and the van in '86, returning to the comfort of another Valiant, a gift from Daddy after an argument where dropping two hundred bucks on six slanted cylinders proved easier for him than saying sorry.

That car bit it in '88. Determined to reattempt hippie-dom, I approached my father with cash and a request: Find me a VW camper.

I suppose the camper top and bonus couch in the back led him to believe I could mistake the half-ton '67 Chevy pickup he delivered for a boxy German home on wheels. To its credit, this machine had but twenty-six thousand original miles, something no mechanic ever believed without closer inspection, at which point piles of money were offered on the spot.

Daddy's mom died in '89 so I gave him the Chevy—peculiar consolation, but hell, I knew he was in love with it. He traded me for a '77 Plymouth wagon with carbon monoxide leak. Driving across the Pennsylvania Turnpike post-funeral, the muffler escaped in the Blue Mountain tunnel. I visualized it ricocheting off wall, penetrating windshield of the (imagined) car behind me, killing a family of five.

Henry was born in '90. Soon after, his father's grandmother gave us an aged LeSabre. Brown beast. When that quit we parked it, commenced to walking.

Hen's dad split in '93. My dad reappeared, returning the pick-up, as much olive branch as means of transport. My mother rode beside him all that way. They took the Greyhound back to Jersey.

About this time, a friend bestowed upon me a decrepit Toyota wagon, spray-painted gold on the outside, red on the inside—cheesy mob movie restaurant on wheels. I sold it for $175 because the Chevy drove better, meant more.

Much as I loved that truck, butt-to-gas-tank proximity left me ever nervous. Too, I got sick of crawling under the hood to adjust slipped links. I gifted it to a carpenter friend. Resumed walking.

Suzy pulled up with the '84 Cressida one day in '96. "Here, have this."

O, Cressida! My friend Kenan calls it "the Lexus of its day." He says mid-eighties National Geographic ads tout it as automotive potentate. Ride baby-bottom smooth. Power windows. Sun-roof! Real stereo—my first.

It was the best car I ever owned, maintained meticulously, oil change dates like a string of onyx beads Magic Markered under the hood. A mere 146,000 on the odometer.

Henry and I used it for luxury. Big trips to the grocery store. We used it for escape. Summer '99 we drove four thousand miles through the worst heat wave of the century. No a/c. Like the Springsteen song we just rolled down the windows (and opened the roof) and let the wind blow back our hair.

Eventually distance trips became distant memories. Oil leak now oil slick. Black exhaust plume obscuring Green Party bumper sticker. U-joint creaking ominously. (Old car owners must learn what sound equals which problem, lest trips to the mechanic turn into trips to the cleaners.)

Time to let go.

I got the line on an '85 Subaru being offered by a kindly, large musician for a song. His dad gave it to him. He loved it, but fit inside, he said, "like a bowling ball in a hatbox."

Handing me the keys he explained, "You gotta jiggle the button to fasten the seatbelt."

I smiled. Such details are the secret language of old car owners, proof of attention paid. Mystery quirks revealed are excellent signs of a new old car worth buying. You don't want to hear, "It runs good." Much better to learn that starting the engine requires lifting butt three inches from seat, twice rapid dash-banging, and Novena recitation before turning the key.

Additionally, he presented The Log—his father's gorgeous typed minutiae along the lines of, "9/15/87 - used wipers today 128.5 slaps. 2,618 slaps left in blades."

Sold already, I took it for a spin anyway. Stick shift. Exciting. Like Mario Andretti would drive, I thought, if Mario Andretti drove a four-cylinder station wagon. Hail dimples textured the red hood—the sort of arty touch my father might emulate. With a hammer.

Ten minutes and thirteen hundreds bucks later it was mine.

Best of all, it has a/c. A decade in Texas and I've not before enjoyed such. We'll miss the sunroof. But Henry is happy for the trade off, wants to run cold air all the time—compensate for countless drives so hot he sagged in a sweat-drenched stupor in the back.

The process of transferring—affection and possessions—has begun. Like many old car owners I suffer chronic pack-ratism. Henry's friends comment in disgust-bordering-awe at the Toyota's contents: empty bottles, newspapers, yoga mats, soccer cones, tennis rackets, hand weights, boogey boards, skates, broken boards and uniforms from Tae Kwon Do. Even an umbrella, though I irrationally fear these.

Camping stuff: collapsible chairs, tent, sleeping bags, lantern, fishing pole, tackle, anoraks—enough gear to set up roadside house in case of breakdown, enough random snack food items and water (officially designated for overheating) to subsist for weeks. Crumpled atlas, outdated business cards, directions to friends' houses. The wobbly-headed dashboard dog (referred to as compass—I have no sense of direction). Not one but two St. Christophers—mandatory safe travel aids.

Eventually Toyota love will fade, give way to Subaru adoration. I hope my son falls particularly hard. No doubt it will be the car he learns to drive in. And, quite possibly, the first in his own series of old faithfuls. (2000)

## HOPE FOUND

Early evening, on the road, I use the falling darkness as an excuse to stop, though we haven't traveled near as far as I'd hoped on day one of our journey. I also stop here because of the sign: Welcome to Hope, Arkansas. Hours ago we whizzed right on by Faith (Texas). But we cannot afford to pass up Hope.

We need hope, Henry and I. It has been a hellish year and in this, the final week of 1997, we have—well, I have—decided flight is more appropriate than fight anymore.

Henry is seven. Excepting my brief, recent marriage, we have been alone together since just before he turned two.

Late on Christmas night, the eve of our departure from Austin, the only hometown he ever remembers having, my son laid on my big bed and wept until he shook.

"I don't want to leave here," he stuttered, between gasps. I understood perfectly, absolutely was enraged to the core myself that we were being driven out. But I feigned confidence. Had no choice.

"Honey, I'm sorry. But I promise you, where we're going is wonderful, too. I'm sorry we have to go. But Mommy made a mistake. We all do sometimes. And now, we have to fix that. We have to be safe."

*To be safe.* To escape the devastation of sleepless nights and constant looking-over-of-shoulder daily incurred by being stalked, I have decided we must run away. Not the first time in my life.

I'd run from my father at eighteen. Run from bad boyfriends and worse jobs in the sixteen years since. And though I had not stopped then to analyze why, precisely, I was running, this time was different. This time, before going I knew the reason for going. Knew the very same thing had sent me packing again and again. Fear.

Those other times, I would not voice it. Could not recognize or acknowledge it. Now the fear flashed in my mind like some neon welcome sign at the gates of hell. One man had built this sign. But a million other fears—great and small, real and imagined—accumulated in thirty-four years, provided the power to make that sign stay lit up around the clock.

My parents, I like to think, meant well as they strove to protect me, to show me the safe way through life. They themselves had run from the fear of a bleak life in South Philly, a city filled with at least as much brotherly hate as love. They'd run to the promise of the crime-free security via small-town life in South Jersey, built a home from scraps and surrounded it with a hedgerow. To keep out. To keep out the strangers and nosy neighbors and noise and evil that was out there.

And it was out there. We knew about it even as we fought against it. They told us all about it. Let the evil in in snippets.

Back in the old days there were only one or two papers and maybe a single nightly newscast. But in my time spent behind that shrubbery wall, and then in the years after I left, they added to the collection.

In forty-five years of marriage my parents have scrutinized the *Philadelphia Inquirer,* the *Philadelphia Daily News,* the *Philadelphia Bulletin,* the *Courier Post,* the *Gloucester County Times.* There was, eventually, TV news available at noon and six and eleven. *Time, Newsweek, Reader's Digest.* Then came CNN.

And from these sources filtered down reports of the infinite sources of danger out there. Certain things, many things, had to be avoided. And in avoiding them, we would remain safe. From everything except the fear.

I will never forget Dolores Dellapenna. I wonder now if anyone else but her parents and me recall her. Dolores was kidnapped from a trolley in Philly, murdered, chopped to bits, mailed home, one piece at a time. I think I was seven, a new reader, when I caught the fever of scouring the papers for the bad news. Read each night the latest gruesome detail in the story.

I figured out quickly to analyze this and other reports of horror. Knew to map out all of the possible things that led to Dolores' death. I could fear murderers. That was easy. But what else? Going out alone? Living in a city? Getting on a trolley?

My parents warned me of everything, fortifying admonishment with footnotes culled from their sources. If you leave home, you will be killed. A man will be waiting for you. A big man. A black man. A man with a gun. He will grab you and hurt you and torture you and rape you and kill you. Slowly. He might not even mail you home.

There were the smaller things, too. Less threatening, perhaps, in the big picture. But potential freak accidents were not to be laughed at. Look here. This man got his leg chopped off in an escalator mishap. My God! Did you see what that tornado did to those poor people's home? Don't get near that toaster with wet hair. And of course, the most famous of all: If you lean back in your chair, you'll fall backwards, break your neck and die. *It happened to my friend's sister back in '53.*

The fear caught me, captured me, tormented me. I ventured out, dared it more and more as I entered adulthood. But foolishly so. Liquid courage was a favorite. Drunk, everything seemed a little less scary, if only for a few hours. Strangers seemed less foreboding. One-night stands safe. Driving, wasted, at three A.M. down streets unknown, rational.

Those days, I blocked the fear of legitimate danger. But I could not fully block the general fear. I would recoil at the thought of plugging in an appliance, remembering still the shock of my toddler fingers making contact with an outlet. I refused to carry umbrellas. Shrunk away from anything but familiar food. Avoided revolving doors at all costs.

Until the jolt. When real fear came to my door, walked through it, climbed in my bed, slept beside me at night. When I realized that terror might not hold the key to my heart but nonetheless had one to my front door. When that clicked, I ran. Fast and far.

I did not set out with any intention other than hiding, of

keeping this thing, this man, from finding me. But, quite by accident I stumbled along the way into facing my fears head-on. Not just the man fear. All of the fears.

More days than not I felt paralyzed emotionally, the prognosis for ever walking again, let alone walking with confidence, a bleak-to-nil possibility. Some days I shut my mind totally, could not bear to fathom the work I needed to do to learn to crawl, to toddle, to move toward moving through the fear, fear, fear.

When I left, so many people told me I was brave and I was strong and they had not seen such courage in me before. Not the first time I'd been accused of strength when I felt nothing but weakness. Like the shy woman chattering away at a party, over-compensating for the pain of self-consciousness and sense of isolation, I sent out some incorrect message that I was bold.

But I was not strong. Or, if I was, I was far too busy focusing on the fear to see any fortitude that might lie within.

And then I got to Knoxville, Tennessee, my destination for escape. And slowly, the view became clearer.

But Austin is a long way from Knoxville. A two-day drive if you push it hard. And before Knoxville there was Faith and Hope and a thousand other little places to get through.

We pull into a hotel, some national chain deal, that night in Hope. The clerk steps forward. She appears to be roughly eighteen, still groping with a budding fashion sense. Her bright red faux–business suit is trimmed in even fauxer-leopard skin fur. We exchange information and money. She hands me my key card.

"Where can I get a beer around here?" I am exhausted but know from driving long distance before that I will be too wired to sleep without chemical assistance.

"You can't."

"I can't?"

"This is a dry county."

I had forgotten this about the South—odd liquor laws, scattered unpredictably. I do not want to believe her and so, adopting that loud, slow talk typically reserved for foreigners and the elderly, I try again, increasing the volume.

"Not anywhere? No bar?" My brain isn't working well. Some incorrect signal is coming in, telling me if I try long enough or loud enough she will reach under the counter and extract a six pack of something really cheap and awful and sickly sweet and share it with me.

"You'd have to drive back fifteen miles to the closest liquor store."

I do the math. Thirty miles round trip for a cocktail. Not worth it.

I saunter away, drive Henry around to our room. He is still shaken at the prospect of moving, but distracted momentarily by an opportunity to jump on the beds and check out the cable TV, a treat only available to him on the road.

I look at the menu provided for the greasy spoon adjacent to the hotel. Call up and order us some grilled cheese sandwiches, some home fries prepared, as they only are in the South, scattered, covered, smothered—that is, with onions and cheese and plenty of unidentifiable (animal? vegetable? mineral?) yellow liquid oil.

"Can you bring it to my room?" I ask the voice on the other end. A seemingly simple question, but just ordering has taken ten minutes of being put on hold, picked back up, put on hold again.

"Well, we're kinda busy down here and I'm alone."

I explain that I don't want to leave my son alone—he's already unwinding now, shoes off, TV on, and I do not want to push his frazzled nerves another inch. We negotiate some more. Ridiculously long for such a basic interaction. Finally, she agrees to bring the food to the room, no more than a couple hundred feet from the restaurant.

Thirty minutes pass. Forty-five. I call the restaurant. The waitress sounds irritated. "I thought *you* said *you* were going to pick it up."

Meekly, backing down from her authoritarian voice, I apologize. Make excuses as if maybe I had been confused, though I know beyond a doubt she'd promised to deliver.

"I'm sorry. That's my fault. Maybe I misunderstood."

"Well, I'll go ahead and bring it now," she says and hangs up. Two minutes later, the door knocks. There she stands, daunting, a brown polyester uniform the precise shade of the hair on her upper lip. Again I apologize, tip her amply. Bid her a pleasant night.

The food is cold. And soggy.

"Mom, where are our drinks?"

She has forgotten the Sprites. I panic. Do not want to bother her again. Want to avoid confrontation at all costs. I know I paid for the beverages. But the loss of two dollars vs. facing another annoyed stare stops me from calling her. I rifle through my bag for change, step out to the vending machines.

Machine broken. Me broken. Henry, hearing the news, on the verge of breaking. This is some small but final blow. We are falling apart.

I suck in my breath, pick up the phone, dial the two-digit extension for the restaurant. I am afraid of this woman. Scared she will yell at me, as I have been scared my whole life that any-one I encounter will yell at me.

"Um, I'm really, really sorry to bother you . . ."

"Yes?"

"You forgot our drinks."

"Oh, I did, didn't I?"

No yelling. Just calm acknowledgement.

"I'll bring them right over."

Two more minutes. Another knock at the door. Me, apologiz-ing again and again, explaining how I tried to avoid this, tried the vending machine.

The look in her eyes that had before appeared stern now soft-ens, borders on incredulous. "Honey, you ordered the drinks. You paid for them. I forgot them. They're your drinks. Of course you should call and ask me to bring them. That's your right."

Again I bid her a pleasant evening. Her thirty second speech, its flat out message, succinctly wraps up so much of what I have been trying to learn in therapy. Two dollars worth of soda and a dollar's worth of tip have bought me what thousands of dollars of psychology has only begun to tap into.

Of course I shouldn't have been afraid to call her. Why was I so goddamned scared all the time?

We pull out early the next day, but not before going to the restaurant and confidently ordering breakfast.

And as we drive away, continue our eastward journey, I do not leave Hope behind me. I take the message of Hope with me. I am still petrified. Of the cars around me, of the man behind me, of what lay before us.

Broken, frightened, but trying to reign it in and not pass my fear onto my child, I forge ahead not knowing what to expect. But what I am finding is even the most frightened girls can find courage, can be strong.

And that strength is located in the oddest places.  (1998)


## KNOXVILLE, TENNESSEE

"Miss Gillespie?"

It was afternoon by the time we pulled into downtown Knoxville, my brain instantly flipping to overload, overwhelmed with memories. I was also pretty damn hungover. This man, looking at me through dark sunglasses, speaking my name though I did not know him, heightened the surreality.

"Yep, that's me. You can call me Spike." Later, I found out how he had identified me so easily. Henry and I were the only guests scheduled to arrive that day at the Hotel St. Oliver, a historic building on the Market Square. The man before us was James, the live-in manager. He'd been waiting.

I chose the St. Oliver as our home base for a number of reasons. First and foremost, I had lived here once before, courtesy of a freak series of events—one of those times when drama came calling while I was looking the other way. The first time I ever arrived in Knoxville was in '87 to take an internship with a magazine company. I was assigned to questionable intern housing near the University of Tennessee. Almost immediately, my roommate and I were treated to the sight of a flasher, servicing himself at our open, waist-high living room window.

Recurrent visits by Penis Man led roomie to take action. The company we worked for was at its peak. They blew money out the ass left and right. Our complaints of feeling unsafe were unbelievably rewarded with the announcement that we would be moved, immediately, all expenses paid, to one of the best hotels in the city. Back then it was the Barclay House.

I never did stop laughing at my good fortune, my continental breakfasts, my free daily papers, my maid service for the three months they put us up there. And so, when I set out in '97 to find a place in Knoxville, I asked around, found the Barclay, long closed,

**1 3**

had recently been taken over and reopened by a wealthy old man who owned half the city.

As the St. Oliver, the place was new, under-publicized, and in desperate need of clientele. Weeks before we embarked on our journey, I struck a bargain via phone, arranged to pay a very decent monthly rental fee. Technically, I had no money, not to mention I was still paying rent back in Texas. But I dipped into the funds earmarked for the IRS, threw financial caution to the wind, and signed us up for two months.

I had more practical reasons for choosing the hotel over an apartment. Doing so eliminated the need to set up a phone and utilities, to buy furniture, to sign a lease. And then there was the safety factor, the main reason I had left Austin. The staff had promised me confidentiality, would screen all calls and visitors. They placed us on the top floor, in the back, the odds of running into other potential guests limited. Not to mention the always-locked security bolt on the front door. This was not some Ramada Inn where anyone could wander in off the streets: even access to the lobby was limited to the registered. Round two of feeling safe started the moment I walked through that heavy door.

My god, how the place had changed. James led us into the lobby. Once spotless—functional and efficient but sparse—now it spilled over with gorgeous antique furniture, mirrors, and gilt-framed oil paintings. A little fountain bubbled on the front desk. The proprietor, in keeping with the historic theme, had emptied some of his warehouses full of treasures and filled the two dozen rooms to the rafters with antique furnishings and Persian rugs.

We took the molasses-powered elevator to the third floor, and James showed us our new home. He'd left a treat for Henry there, saved from the New Year's Eve party the night before, a traditional gift from his hometown, New Orleans. In a Crescent City drawl, James told us about the renovations, the future plans, how delighted he was to have us. Then, furthering Henry's growing enchantment, he announced that his dog Sadie lived in the hotel, too, and would simply love the company of a little boy.

I looked around our room, grinned. There in the center stood a king-sized bed, antique four-poster frame, flanked on either side by overstuffed chairs. In the corner, a mint-condition, century-old Italian-crafted desk, polished like a flawless diamond.

Off to the side, the room jutted out a bit: Henry's area. A pull-out couch, portraits of hunting dogs, a delicate curio cabinet. Such a far cry from the beaten, junk shop furniture at home, the posters haphazardly slapped on the wall. Here, I knew, I could live out, at least for a little while, my goofy lifelong dream of being a writer-in-residence.

In real life, I was a recently unemployed woman with no foreseeable income. I was hunted by a psycho. I was battling depression. Trying to both block and process the string of horrors in my immediate wake. But now, if only momentarily, I was a damn princess in a fancy-schmancy setting, some privileged someone on holiday getting away from it all.

Granted, there were drawbacks. The heater didn't quite work and Tennessee winters are a bit more chilly than those in Texas. We compensated with layers of clothes and little ceramic heaters, learning fast enough where the fuse box was, as any extra pull on the building's ancient wiring often blacked out the entire floor.

Then there was the matter of food. James gave us a microwave to set on the tiny counter of the wet bar, an old shelf to use for pantry. But the dorm-size fridge and lack of oven limited us. And so I set out to show Henry the places I had loved to eat, one of them blocks away, two others less than a stone's throw.

The owners of all three places remembered me and gushed over Henry. The cooks at Harold's Delicatessen would emerge from the kitchen to talk to him about basketball. Then Harold himself would be waiting with a piece of candy when my son half-boldly, half-shyly walked to the end of the counter to pay our bill. Back in Austin, I had grown so fearful that letting Henry walk even ten steps away from me in a public place was unthinkable. This little ritual we established at Harold's, these tiny three-minute intervals apart, were in fact a major obstacle overcome. More safeness. More exhaling.

As it happened, there was another time I had returned to Knoxville to collect myself. That time the drama I was dealing with was Henry's pregnancy. My entire second trimester I spent in this healing town. And now Pete, over at Pete's, who'd made me an egg sandwich nearly every day during that time, cooked breakfast for the two of us, laughingly chiding Henry when his eyes proved much bigger than his stomach.

Next stop: The Tomato Head, catty-corner across the square from our hotel, home of the best pizza I've ever had. I'd met the owner, Mahasti, during that pregnancy trip to Tennessee—Henry's father worked with her then. When she opened the Tomato Head, she invited me to read my poetry there. On the walls, Henry pointed to the store's T-shirts, the familiar hand-painted images on each: The work of our friends Kathi and Charlie and Ollie. That place felt more like home than a restaurant, so familiar were the faces and decor.

I *knew* it was right to come back here. *Knew* that voice in my head telling me to run to Knoxville was speaking a truth. And now here was the proof.

Many of my friends here had known James, Henry's dad. Many had known the child in utero, had patted my growing belly. And all of them had good memories to share, kind words to offer. Icing on the cake for the boy who was less homesick by the hour. It had been years since James and I lived in the same town, since he succumbed to alcoholism and lost touch for large chunks of time. How incredible it was to re-visit the memories of an unsick James. How fortifying for a child to meet strangers who were anything but, who could tell him all sorts of good stories about both of his parents.

Immediately I signed us up for library cards—the library in Knoxville is small but inviting, one of my favorite libraries anywhere, also just minutes away from the St. Oliver. In my absence, an entire video section had been added and many cold nights, in the heart of a downtown vacant after business hours, we'd sit and watch movies on the big bed, Sadie curled at Henry's feet, a welcome substitute for our own much-missed dog back at home.

The school year started a few days after we settled in, and with it fear returned. Raised in a racist home in a racist town, I grew up fighting the stereotypes that had been handed to me like daily bread. But here came a test. We were zoned for a school on the East Side. Henry, who had just left a small, ninety percent white school population was about to enter a situation completely reversed. A few friends cautioned me—did I really want to add to his shock by putting him in such an unfamiliar environment? No one made overt racial remarks, but I could hear the worry.

And the worry seized me. Would I be forcing him to be some sort of political statement? It was hard enough entering a new school, mid-year, no friends. Would racism run the other direction now, leave my son ostracized, make the transition unbearable?

As had been the case each other night before each other first day of school, I slept poorly, my son's admitted anxiety paling by comparison to my own. Race was actually the smallest issue that concerned me. Mostly, I was consumed with thoughts of what a stupid, stupid person I was.

I lay awake thinking: If only I hadn't screwed up so bad, put us in such a dangerous position with my hasty choices . . . If only I had thought harder . . . If only . . . then none of this would be happening. We would be back in our same neighborhood, rooted for the duration of his childhood, as I had always hoped and planned.

No. I had to stop thinking like that. This was our reality now. I drove him over to register, sat in the office waiting to get situated. Of course, we didn't have all the necessary paperwork. When they sent us away to get an immunization form, it was me who cried. It had been so hard walking through that door, wondering how Henry would fare so far from his lifelong friends. Now, we had to turn around, deal with red tape, try again.

Take two. Here came the real test. As the none-too-proud "owner" of a restraining order against my ex-husband, I had been through the drill enough times now to steel myself. In Austin, moving from one school to another, I had to explain the situation—the potential danger—to the principal of our new school.

She looked at me, sighed when I told my tale, gave the distinct impression that she really was annoyed to have to deal with us, clearly "problem" people in her eyes. When we discussed security issues, she did nothing to quell my anxiety, instead detailing a kidnapping years before, involving circumstances extremely similar to my own—an ex-stepfather came to steal his ex-stepson. A teacher had intervened and been injured. The principal wanted me to know that, if someone came for my son, her teachers would not intervene, they would wait for the kidnapping to occur, then they would call the police and, if they could, they would try to reach me.

I was incredulous—that this was policy, that she would deliver the information smugly. I tried to convince myself she was just trying to scare me. No, she had succeeded in scaring me. It was that discussion, more than anything, that pushed me to make my decision to flee the state.

When I did withdraw him from that school, the same principal unhesitatingly handed me Henry's file. "I don't want to know where you're going," she said, sternly, clearly glad to be rid of us.

That in mind, I expected the worst from the new administration. Sitting in the office, waiting to register Henry, I caught a glimpse of my reflection in a glass door. It was the drawn look I'd seen on my mother's face times when things were really bad. The exhaustion that wiped me out through '97, from which I'd received a brief respite spending time with Kathi and Steven and dragging my kid to my old stomping grounds, returned full force. Meekly, again frightened at full volume, I began to explain our situation, expecting them to greet my story with disgust, as I'd encountered in Austin.

The women behind the counter looked at me. One by one they shook my hand and then Henry's. I was informed in a tone more like that of a sister than a principal's assistant that I was not to worry. They'd seen plenty of restraining orders in their day. They would do anything they could to help. Now I really had to fight back the tears. This was more than I dreamed of, validation that I wasn't crazy, that that other principal *had* further victimized me for being a victim of stalking. I could not thank them enough.

That afternoon, Henry told me he'd had a fine, fine day. Did I realize that his school had *the only* unicycle team in all of Tennessee? Not only that, but a counselor had pulled him aside. I suppose giving our address as a hotel suggested we were transient in a traditional way—like people forced to live in shitty hotels, flophouses. How could these people, in this poor, segregated neighborhood guess that I was home that day sitting in a Queen Anne chair, typing away at my antique desk? The counselor told my son that if we needed housing, food, anything, all we had to do was ask.

That evening, as it happened, the school was scheduled for a field trip to see the Harlem Globetrotters at the city coliseum. It was too late for Henry to join the group, but I bought us a couple of tickets, hoping to assimilate him quickly.

At half-time, out came the local entertainment. Yes. One unicycle team, in fact *the only* unicycle team in all of Tennessee. Henry's new classmates. They rolled around the floor, crashed, got up, rolled around some more. He was amazed. He was proud. He wasn't going to make me take him back to Texas anytime soon.

Not long after that, I returned one morning from dropping him off, parked my car, got out and headed toward the hotel. It was raining, dark and cold. A man came toward me, moving fairly rapidly, and I froze. He was saying something to me. I couldn't hear what, but I was terrified. Post Traumatic Stress in full gear. Since the stalking began, all men scared me. I took a deep breath, reminded myself I wasn't in Texas, this wasn't my ex. My voice, small whisper, "Excuse me?"

"I said, it's raining, would you like to share my umbrella?"

The culmination of little kindnesses—understanding school administrators, an adoring hotel manager, a stranger offering to shield me from the rain—melted something inside of me. I had no false hope that I could ever again totally let down my guard. But slowly, the glacier inside shifted, made room for ideas that the stalking had relegated to a small corner of my mind. Not everyone was out to get me. There were places I could go where it was still safe to walk down the street. (1998)

## REMEMBER THE WOOLWORTH'S

I proudly sport, on the back of my '67 Chevy pickup, a bumper sticker that is as goofy as it is true. *I Wasn't Born in Texas*, it proclaims, *But I Got Here as Fast as I Could.* People ask where I got it. Well . . .

As it happened, my parents, who've ventured out of the tri-state area comprised of New Jersey, Delaware, and Pennsylvania, perhaps ten times in their collective 125 years on the planet, decided one day to take a little drive down to Austin to see me and their darling grandson, Hank. In fact, the occasion of this trip was to bestow upon me the Chevy, a vehicle my father and I have passed back and forth in a sort of Freudian fashion for the past eight years or so.

It was my turn to be on the receiving end of this blessing/curse, and so it was, like a slow boat to Texas, they wound their way down to my neighborhood. Since Austin is a bit closer to San

Antonio than is New Jersey, and since they are retired and have time to kill, and since most travelers like to test the patience of their hosts, my folks decided to stick around for awhile, and to . . . ahem . . . "let" me take them to see the Alamo.

Oddly, and as an aside, we couldn't take the truck, seeing as the seat belt situation would not allow for four of us to be strapped in at once. Therefore, I borrowed my roommate's Toyota for the occasion, praying as we piled in that my holy-rolling father would not notice her bumper. Upon which was stuck a pro-choice bumper sticker.

Bear in mind, please, my father started his own one-man picket line before the ink dried on the Roe v. Wade decision. If he saw this thing on her car, I just knew it would no longer be a bumper sticker, it would be a beating heart, more specifically his beating heart—pulsing with bloody hatred for anyone associated with anything pro-choice.

Which would be my roommate. And which would be me. (Even if I wasn't pro-choice, which I am, I would have been guilty by association with that bumper sticker.) Of course, he had spotted it, immediately, but said nothing at first, waiting, instead, to offer his insight as we were barreling south on IH-35, me breaking my normal driving speed of thirty miles per hour.

I nearly lost control of the car when he said, his cigar clenched firmly betwixt toothless gums, "I saw watcher girlfrenz got on the back," in the thick Jersey brogue I myself had spent years unacquiring.

My hands, not having once left the ten o'clock/two o'clock position, wrestled fiercely to keep us on the road. I made what I hoped was a face that indicated I was far too busy focusing on safe driving to have heard his words, despite the fact he was spilling out of his bucket seat and partially into mine, his lips mere inches from my ears.

At this point, we were a good two miles outside of Austin and the first act was promising for some very thrilling plot turns. I was not disappointed.

Though the Alamo itself bored my parents instantly—they could not believe anything in Texas might be small, especially a place like this, a place with a gigantic if questionable reputation. My son concurred via a temper tantrum—the sort of which he only and ever throws around people who see him just occasionally. Still, we were in San Antonio already, and decided to try out a few other tourist activities.

I lagged back with my mother, who'd recently had her knee replaced, as my father barreled along the River Walk, again growing fast disgruntled. You know, that old New Jersey way of thinking—*Hell, if you're going to put a bunch of shops together, you should go ahead and put them in a mall for Pete's sake.*

All hope was not lost, however, as we at last spotted a place of great interest and excitement—the San Antonio Woolworth's. As have been Woolworth's since the beginning of time, this one, too, was chock-full of fascinating items available only at thousands of other Woolworth's.

My mother and I took the child off to find him some cute T-shirt—you know, *My Grandparents Went to Texas and All I Got Was This Lousy T-Shirt and An Old Chevy*—while my father drifted elsewhere.

Our task completed, we went back to find Pop, stopping only once to size up a rack of acrylic Davy Crockett 'coonskin caps. We spotted him just as he was crouching down to move a big box. Curious—had he procured a job as stock boy in the minutes we'd been gone?—we approached him to see what was up.

He employed a series of grunts and gestures—his preferred method of communication—to indicate there was, a few feet away, a small black-and-white TV set, the one and only "major" appliance apparently for sale in the whole place. He further indicated, by plopping down on the box which he had angled just so, that he intended to watch this TV.

At last, he spoke some real words. *Honey, get me the game.*

Though I had no idea what he was talking about, Mom snapped to attention. She hobbled toward the set and fiddled with the antennae, bringing in a very grainy picture of the World Series. Finally, it dawned on me, "his" team, the Phillies, was going for the pennant.

I was mortified, certain that people would notice I was somehow related to this crazy man. And so, when he made one final gesture, and muttered something about us disappearing for awhile so he could watch in peace, I gladly obliged. I shuffled behind my limping mother, my child slung on my hip, causing me to walk with a gait similar to hers, the whole while wondering whatever happened to all those lectures he'd given us about what the neighbors will think.

Mom and Hank and I killed about forty-five minutes at a Burger King. Not once did she mention my father's behavior. She wasn't one whit embarrassed. Clearly, from her quick and nimble television adjustments, she'd had years of practice which left her either unaffected or maybe tolerant or maybe even proud, I really couldn't tell. At last, when our dictated hour of banishment drew to a close, we headed out for a synchronized hobble back to the Woolworth's.

Upon my second entrance, I spotted the rack of bumper stickers. Perhaps they caught my eye because now I actually had a bumper to stick things to. I flipped through, passing over anything slightly subtle or remotely inspirational. And then I found it, tacky and true.

*I Wasn't Born in Texas, But I Got Here as Fast as I Could.*

Pleased with my dollar well spent, I wandered back toward the TV "department," fully expecting to find my mother and son, who'd gone on ahead, weeping because some manager informed them my father had been carted off to prison or for mental evaluation.

Instead, I found my father, relaxing on that box of coffee cups, surrounded by a crowd of strangers. There he sat, Mr. I-Was-Born-In-Philly-Pal-So-Don't-Tell-Me, lending loud commentary to the eager ears of countless baseball fans.

I can't exactly recount for you much of the Alamo, but I assure you, I'll never forget the Woolworth's.    (1996)


## ROAD TRIP

Geese are flying over the snowy prairie, trying to get it together, form a V. I bust out one of my favorite corny jokes.

"You know how, when you see that formation, one side is sometimes longer than the other?" I ask Erik, seated beside me, driving us home. I try to sound scientific.

Erik doesn't know. "Because there are more geese on one side!" I'm sure I'm shouting, shout being my normal volume.

Erik can't resist one upping me. He wants to discuss this. Only when he opens his mouth to speak, it's not the calm, deep Erik voice I know. Instead, it is one of several politically incorrect alter-egos that lurks within him, emerging regularly as we barrel from Kansas to Austin.

"Greater than, lesser than!" this dim character proclaims in a funny voice, gesturing wildly at the geese who have by now managed to resemble the sign for greater than.

My son Henry, sprawled in the back seat, wrapped in sleeping bags to deal with the sub-freezing temperature and hardly adequate car heater, begins to laugh. "Stop it," I say. To Erik. To Henry. "This is so incorrect." But I'm laughing, too. I'm laughing hardest of all. Henry is laughing at least as much at me as the joke.

We need to laugh. Six days ago, Henry and I set out alone, to tackle the distance from Austin to St. Louis, to see his dad, whom he has not seen in over a year.

We drove straight into the ice storm formerly known as Oklahoma. The distance passed slowly as we crawled and slid, 35 MPH, along a highway so treacherous I could not speak, could only think, seriously, any minute might be our last. The only sound I made, gripping the wheel, silently begging the universe to spare us, came from my back. You could hear the knots forming, tying up my muscles like some macramé project gone awry.

On rare gas stops, the only time I could speak, I promised my son. *It will be better on the way back.* On the way back, we'll have Erik.

Erik caught a lift north ahead of us. In the interest of helping us out, he agreed to share the drive back if I would pick him up in Kansas.

During a phone call to firm up our schedule, I let him in on a fantasy I've been harboring, involving him.

"When I see you," I teased, "Can I . . . just ride in the back with the crayons and paper?"

"Sure," he says.

Driving across what looks like ocean foam—dry snow blowing across the thankfully clear highway 70—to meet my co-pilot, I worry. This is worse than preparing for a first date. I want so much from this man, a man new to my life. I want safe passage. I want to not find out he has some chronic gas problem or has a need to listen to bad music, cranked up, while driving. I want to believe I won't drive him insane, to the point he leaps from the moving car, with my sometimes need to talk too much, too fast, too loud.

I chastise myself. Stop hoping for so much. This is the perfect metaphor for my life. I always expect too much. He'll probably drive too fast. He'll probably let me down.

He does not. He smiles, waving at us as we turn down Tennessee Avenue in Lawrence, Kansas, into the driveway. I blurt out the line I've been rehearsing, which is sincere if not spontaneous. "No one has ever been so happy to see you."

"Me?" he says, and flashes that grin which is, happily, just as I'd recalled it, equal parts sly and humble, sexy and nonchalant. "You look good," he says. I know it's not true. I look awful. I'm still a nervous wreck from my harrowing storm experience. But this is how he is, what prompted me to propose a twelve-hour drive with a man I hardly know. I knew enough from our chats in my kitchen, the way he talks to my kid. He is Mister Laid Back, Mister Get the Job Done, Mister Make Others Feel Good.

A Virgo, he insists on repacking my slob-job, somehow making fit, like an intricate puzzle, our bags and emergency supplies, his bags and drum kit. I plop into the passenger side and begin to knit. And talk. And talk.

It works. He talks too. He teaches me about 7/4ths time and Metallica's drummer. I pull out my best old stories of past loves and growing up because he has never heard them before. We discuss love and sex and hopes and dreams: past, present, future. His music is good—stuff from his own bands included. He doesn't complain about mine.

Miraculously, though we are new to driving together, we pull off some of those un-awkward long silences, too, the kind that take other companions years to master. All the while his eyes are steady on the road. He drives the speed limit. Uses his turn signal.

Though he'd feigned pain when I confessed I am one of those people—I honk at markers: city limits, county limits, state lines— at one point he hits the horn repeatedly. "Are we in a new place?" I ask.

"Not yet. Couple of miles. I'm just practicing."

My macramé back unknots itself as the miles unfold, night falls, and I sit back, wheel clenching unnecessary, gazing at the bright stars above. (2001)

I've been to L.A. twice. Once as a fledgling reporter to profile Howie Mandel for the cover of a prototypical magazine that never did make it to the newsstands. And the second time for one of those drunken Kerouacian tours all writers must take at some point, feigning to find themselves. That time, I hung out long enough to hike illegally up to the HOLLYWOOD sign, get loaded at the Gaslight, have my guitar and boombox ripped off, and procure a small tattoo of a cow and the slogan *Born To Graze* on my right bicep, courtesy of Little John down at the Sunset Strip Tattoo Parlor.

These events, while amusing in retrospect, did not come close to giving me a real taste for that inimitable attitude associated with residents of the City of Angels, that arrogance people like me mostly just read about in *People*. No, my true descent into the pit of snobbery was several more years in the making.

In fact, I met Hollywood not in L.A., but rather on neutral territory. Thanks to tenuous connections and the absurdity of electronic love, a few years ago I found myself romantically linked with Barry, who had recently transformed himself from poor-son-of-an-East-coast-rabbi to successful-West-coast-screenwriter with the sale (for a half-mil) of his first script. A generous man, Barry used his newfound fortune to woo me. And I, despite my hardcore feminist, dutch-date morals, allowed him to share. He supplied the plane tickets and hotel rooms. I dished out the gratuitous sex. And best of all, we really liked each other. A lot. Casting couch? Hardly. Sure, I wanted him to look at the one screenplay I'd written (poorly) and offer tips. But even if he'd refused, I'd not have kicked him out of the bed he financed.

Date one was Vegas—the Hard Rock Hotel. Date two, Austin, my turf. Date three, he called to inform me, like Charlie with a new exciting assignment for his angel, was to commence in San Francisco. Barry admitted up front that this was more than romance. Three other couples would be joining us, and he wanted to make a good impression. Was I up to the task?

Having grown up in a household of eleven, I admit I never

did get over my aversion to crowds, to having to plan for groups bigger than two. But I can be a good sport when pressed. Particularly when pressed with the promise of good food, endless booze, expenses paid, and a chance to pretend to be someone I am not.

There were a few rules—I could feel Barry squirming on his end of the line as he made this clear. First, could I please avoid reference to my latest tattoo, a rather large back piece that was still in the healing process? Second, he wasn't sure how to put this and certainly it wasn't that he didn't enjoy my bawdiness in private, but, um . . . well these folks were a bit conservative, two were from rather religious backgrounds and um. . . ? You want me to act like a lady, an L.A. lady, foxy lady? I sang, cutting to the proverbial chase. Yes. Yes, that was it.

I pack the two dresses I own but balk at buying shoes to replace my combat boots. Let them deal. A friend takes me to the drugstore and selects for me a variety of makeup products, grand total less than ten bucks. We practice application. I board my flight.

I meet them, en masse, for the first time, in the Tiki Room, a shitty restaurant in the basement of the most pricey hotel in the most pricey neighborhood in the city. We shake hands all around: Jake and Christina, they of huge Texas trust funds (are there any other kind?) and non-specific reasons for living the L.A. life. Bill and Jennifer, sharing that lookalike, tall, blonde, fit look, both affable enough, neither jumping out as memorable. And then . . . then . . . Barry introduces me to *them*.

I'd listened to him go on and on about Stacy, son of one of those famous ancient crooners, and his little trophy wife Charity. Stacy this and Stacy that and . . . okay, Barry, great. My hunch that Stacy will be far less than promised is right on target. His wife— they're newlyweds—clings to him like shit on a shingle, careful not to entangle the fifty-thousand-carat atrocity on her finger in his Bobby Sherman hair. Stacy, despite his questionable rank in the Hollywood food chain—as he explains, he "sort of produces stuff"—has that air of self-importance which he clearly hopes will project the message: *"Look, my father's fame has nothing to do with it. I'm fabulous because I'm me and you'll respect me for the same reason."*

Dinner proceeds awkwardly as I fight to keep myself in check, despite an overwhelming desire to spew the word "bullshit" every time Stacy opens his mouth. A particularly bad cover band comprised of clearly bored members floats on a movable dock around the pond, created for just this purpose, in the center of the room. From time to time a pseudo-rainstorm pours down from the ceiling, threatening to electrocute our entertainers. The audience loves it but I can't figure out if this is due to the schlock factor or in spite of it. When all is said, done, and consumed, I watch the four men among us melodramatically race to whip out their platinum cards, to one up each other, to "impress the ladies." Out of respect for Barry, I force my eyes not to roll back into my head.

Day two finds us dining at an equally shitty restaurant, this time in Marin, the exorbitant prices no doubt rationalized as rent for our bayside table. I look around me at my L.A. contingent. I have dressed up (in my mind) and they have clearly dressed down (in theirs). Appropriately enough, we are all wearing clothes from the Gap. I keep my irony to myself.

As it happens, we are traveling cram-packed into a rental minivan. Stacy insists on the role of pilot. And then the fun begins. *Where shall we go?* is the question. The answer much less simple. I told you, I hate groups. They mock-bicker in the parking lot until, frustrated, I suggest we all drop acid and check out the Exploratorium. Juvenile joke, granted, but put forth in hopes of comic relief. I feel my date wince. I smile innocently in return.

The Presidio, we must find the Presidio decide the men. Where *is* the Presidio we wonder as we unwittingly drive all around and through it. Stacy grows increasingly frustrated. I grow increasingly amused. At last it is determined that we will never find this clump of trees. So we exit the Presidio and come up with a new plan. *How about a drive down the crookedest street in the world! Now that sounds like fun! And we'll have lots of company on account of the fact it's a Saturday. Cool!*

We get in line, cars bumper-to-bumper, to take a drive that could be achieved on foot in one-fiftieth the amount of time. Stacy, in a moment of fluster, shifts. Only this is not a stick shift, our vehicle of pleasure. No, this is an automatic. He hits the gas. We smash into the car behind us, a brand new Nissan. Stacy pretends not to notice. In fact, he pretends not to notice the entire ride down the crookedest street. He averts his eyes from the rearview. He maintains his superior sense of superiority. At any moment I expect his arm to come swinging back over the seat, telling us to quiet down, damn it, or he's going to turn this car around. (The kind Nissan driver, no doubt feeling Stacy's evil vibe and not wanting to deal, kindly turn the other way when at last we reach the bottom, an hour later.)

After, thankfully, splitting up for a few hours, we meet back at the hotel to ready ourselves for dinner at Boulevard, one of the more elegant culinary offerings in a city full of elegant culinary offerings. Ignoring Stacy as we mill around the bar waiting to be seated, I focus on the fragile Christina, as she sips her Kir Royale and explains her version of being a housewife—managing the domestic help back in California by cell phone from her gilt- and marble-laden hotel rooms on the continent.

At last, our table ready, we stumble to the darkened bowels of Boulevard, where I have the dubious pleasure of being seated next to Stacy. And here, finally, I get to witness the Hollywood I'd until now only read about, told myself the accounts must be exaggerated, couldn't imagine anyone being that big of an asshole. I sit, buzzed enough to attempt to subtly provoke Stacy. I whisper to him that I have a big new tattoo I'm not supposed to discuss. I launch into refined versions of my liberal feminist manifestos. He smiles nervously at Barry's taste in women.

The food arrives and I admire my order, the way the salmon flakes on my fork and melts in my mouth, the extravagance of having snow crab mashed into my potatoes, the brightness and crispness of the asparagus balanced, as if by top-notch prop masters, like pick-up sticks on a plate that cost more than all my dishes back home put together.

The son of the crooner is less satisfied. A food runner places his bloody entree before him. He scrutinizes. He glares. He clears his throat and in a decidedly non-crooning fashion lashes out. "What happened to our *real* waiter?" he hisses. "Did she leave or something?" The food runner stands and takes it politely, as he is paid two dollars an hour to do. "Sir? Is there a problem?"

*"YES THERE'S A PROBLEM! LOOK AT THIS!"* he points to his plate, the picture-perfect vision of gourmet. We wait, seven forks poised mid-air, for his complaint. "I ordered this with *NO CHEESE.* Do you *HEAR ME? LOOK AT THIS!"*

We all look. And then, we look closer. At last we spot it—

melted perfectly atop a mushroom garnish the size of a quarter is the offensive, dime-size square of dairy product. The food runner apologizes profusely. Charity clings harder to her man, trying to console his offended sensibilities to no avail. His glare screams out, "Don't you *realize* that *I* am the son of a famous, ancient crooner?!!! That I sort of produce stuff?!!"

The plate is removed. I order another unnecessary drink, excusing myself before it arrives. Timidly, I approach the waiters station, a place far more familiar to me in restaurants than any linen-covered table. And I confess: "I am so sorry. I don't really know that guy. I just met him. Please, won't one of you join me outside? I really need a smoke."

They decline. But they smile, gratefully. They are not allowed to mingle with the privileged guests. Or maybe, they just don't care to.

I smile back. I know just how they feel. (1998)

# WHERE WE FIND GOD

## EASTER SUNDAYS

### HOLY SATURDAY, 1997

After spending Holy Thursday and Good Friday in the company of a bearded, thirty-three-year-old Jew (who saves people by helping them get divorced before they kill each other), I collapse into bed late at night. *Finally*, I think, *eight solid hours of sleep.*

But The Holy Child, my only son, has risen early. It is what? Two A.M.? Three A.M.? I am too groggy to even tell. *Mom*, he says, *I sort of threw up a little in my bed. I'm sick.*

*Lie here beside me*, I say, too tired to check his bed—a move I will regret once I do.

*Mom*, he says, rolling over an hour later and poking my arm, *it's me again. I'm going to throw up.* We're off to the bathroom. I watch. I wait. Nothing.

Furball-about-to-fly noises from beside me. Now it is five A.M. *Mom, mom* . . . the urgent cry is interrupted by a gagging noise. *NOT ON THE BED, HONEY! The floor, the floor.*

I spend the next hour cleaning up the floor. Cleaning up my son's mess and the puppy's mess, for in his disrupted sleep, Satch, too, has decided to contribute, has upon the hardwoods shat. *Holy projectiles*, I think.

Four hours, fifty crackers, one Sprite, and two teaspoons of Pepto-B later, the son has risen yet again. He seems fine. So we go to the hardware store. I need three keys I say to the man. My son interrupts, *Mom, Mom!* We don't quite make it out the front door.

This is a swank hardware store, a yuppie haven. Most people turn their heads at the sight of me kneeling before my son, the paper towels I have procured from the cranky clerk now soaked in my hands. He retches. I mop. We are a sight.

### GOOD FRIDAY, 1975

I am twelve and I want so badly for the Holy Spirit to descend upon me in a flash of light or lightning. I want to be Teresa, the

Little Flower, a teen literally dying to see the Lord, swept up in a storm of devoted bliss and hacking TB. I am the youngest lector at our little church, named St. Ann's for the mother of Mary, the Virgin. The other kids cut. Not me. I go. I listen. I wonder.

It is Good Friday and there is a service—three long hours to commemorate Christ's time on the cross. Not at St. Ann's, though. Another church—we have seven in this little town. And this is the one day of the year—What does Jesus have to do, *die* for God's sake?—all join together to commemorate the suffering Christ.

This is not a holy day of obligation. No one says I have to go. But I want to. I want to feel. I want to believe.

I walk there. It's a cloudy day and I am pretty sure every Good Friday of my life has been overcast, or has become overcast at the strike of three P.M., the moment the Lord muttered, "It is finished," and then breathed his last upon that wooden cross.

I listen to the readings. I sit upon the hard wooden bench. I know the stories inside and out, Simon helping to carry the cross. Peter betraying his best friend thrice. Judas—oh that evil, evil man.

At some point, a man comes and sits beside me. It is Daddy. This is a good setting for the two of us. Silence is required and even this early in my life we have nothing to say to each other, so we sit, doing just that. He leaves after awhile.

When it is over, I walk home, across the playground of my elementary school, the little blue skirt my mother sewed for one of my sisters, now passed down to me, flapping in the March wind. It has elastic in the waist and flares a little at the bottom. It doubles as my cheerleading skirt when, no thanks to coordination, but much thanks to my loud mouth and my best friend's status as cheerleader captain, I am picked for the squad.

### EASTER SUNDAY, 1983

I am in college now. Nineteen. A virgin thinking I'll stay that way until I marry. I'm fifteen hundred miles away from the parents who made me go to church. My faith has waned. Still, I go to Mass. I drink all night Saturday night then drag my butt out of bed Sunday and get on my bicycle and ride miles in the Florida heat. Because I don't like the campus chapel and if I'm going to go, I'm going to go to a place I can tolerate.

But can it tolerate me? By now I am, at least on the outside, a punk rock girl. I have a crew cut and lots of metal in my ears. Because I travel by bicycle I am not, as are most women, wearing a frilly dress this day.

Easter is a big day for the hypocrites who turn out, pardon the pun, en masse, to show off for each other and God. Because of this crowd and because I am a little late, I am relegated to "spillover Mass" held in the gym, across the parking lot from the real church. I take a seat in the back. One by one the four members of the two couples in front of me turn, take in my appearance, nudge each other, snicker. They are good, clean-cut Americans, with proper Easter hair and clothes. I have never seen them at Mass before.

I leave afterwards, disgusted. It is Easter Sunday, a day to start again, and the little faith I have left in the Catholic church drains from me like stigmata.


## GOOD FRIDAY, 1986

I am living in sin with Loser Boy. I can barely stand him anymore. I am no longer Catholic though that is a BIG JOKE. Because once they get you and dip you in the water that first month, once they drag you to mass over and over and tell you how you are going to hell and God is punishing you for being bad all the time, well— you just drown in it forever.

I am lying on the mattress on the floor beside the Loser and he wants to have sex. And I can't. And I think it's because today is Good Friday. This does not set well with him.

We drive to the mall, have a fight, and he leaves me. Or I leave him. Walking home in the hellish heat, I spot a man in a wheelchair and he is struggling, cannot control his limbs, is going nowhere slow. Real slow. I offer to push him.

As I do he tells me about Nam, his words twisted in his mouth, crucial information lost to the wind and passing traffic. I push and push and I am dying in this heat. And one block from his home, there is road construction and we cannot access his street. We have to turn around, and detour a million more miles. I can't stand this anymore, but when finally I leave him, mission accomplished, at least I am feeling like Jesus would have approved.

Back at home, I lie back down on the lumpy mattress beside Loser Boy and I feel where the sun burned my face. And I look up at the three-paddled ceiling fan whirling around and around. It is the crucifix and I have found the Lord, as I do every Holy Week, whether I am looking, or looking away.

## GOOD FRIDAY, 1992

It's been so many years now. The memory of the solemn fifth grade me in the cheerleading skirt makes me want, for reasons beyond my comprehension, to go to church this day.

I think I want to test something. I have always felt some sort of faith these years, if not precisely in God. I want to see what triggers I can pull stepping into the place I once left in anger. I walk a mile to St. Ignatius—I love the fiery name. Entering, I see a few people, most of them old, alone, clicking away at their rosary beads.

There is a big wooden cross up at the altar and a woman flitting around it and another woman over by the organ. I am puzzled. Usually, this is a day of silence, or else readings of the Crucifixion. These women lack reverence. Has something changed?

Then I hear the organ lady. She must not know her mike is on. She is snarling, booming orders at the others in a very un-Christian way. I realize: this is a rehearsal for Sunday. They couldn't wait until after three. I am disappointed. I walk around and look at the stations of the cross. I leave.

Walking the mile back to my house, a man pulls up next to me. Do I want to hop in and fuck him? *Do I? Do I?*

I tell him to screw himself. I know Jesus would've said something else. I don't care.

## HOLY SATURDAY, 1997

Here I am again. Last night the children watched a movie about a dog that comes back from the dead. And I thought, *Well, dog spelled backwards is . . .* and then: *Never mind* and *Stop it. Stop looking for these things.*

But they find me. On this Holy Saturday, a homeless boy I know—now thankfully off the streets—stops by. I have not seen him in two years. He asks how I've been and I say crappy. He kneels down and kisses my feet. It's odd. Later I hear he's considering becoming a priest.

Some people fail to find the humor in my *Jesus Christ Super-star* on the answering machine and my crosses on the wall and the portrait of Henry and me as the Mother and Child and the plastic mini Pieta on the bookcase and the prayer of St. Francis on the wall and my fixation with these Holy days.

Once, the son of a rabbi asked me what was up with all the Catholic stuff in my house. Is it a joke or what? I can't answer that.

I can never embrace it again. I can never let it go. Jesus is everywhere and I know it. On my Elton John album, in my bathroom, on my T-shirts, and in my mind.

I spent the week working on a garden. Nothing big. Nothing elaborate. I didn't have the time or the patience. But I couldn't stop myself. They taught me ever since way back that this is the week of new life.

I just had to start some of my own.                               (1997)

## BROKEN MIRRORS

The reflection was shattered. Perhaps not the first time in my life, but surely the most jagged, shards of me scattered at my feet.

I could hardly bear to look down, to catch a glimpse of these pieces of me glinting up, daring me to try to put it back together. Again.

When the mirror is smashed, I have learned, you have to be careful in any attempts to re-assemble. You must acknowledge that no matter what success you have in trying, no matter how closely you piece things back together, the image will never again be the same.

In the past, I would race through the healing process. Not recognizing all the resources available, I too often chose glue that was cheap, the mercuried-glass mosaic slapped together fast, whole blocks of it falling down again and again in chunks. The patterns they left open—these blanks—were recognizable. And though they were not pretty, I somehow took comfort in familiarity.

Last year, though, the whole mirror, what was left of it, crashed to the ground. There was, it seemed, not one thing that could go right. Twice my body failed me, twice I had surgery to remedy this. There were lawyers—God, so many lawyers—as legal battles I never dreamed of emerged. And then there was the emotion.

Depression is an odd beast. No longer denied its existence, still an odd stigma remains. Those of us who suffer it, who've suffered it forever, hate to categorize it for the mental illness it is. Still, somewhere in the back of our minds we cannot deny the effects. Those of us wrestled to the ground by cyclical depression fight valiantly—like St. Michael and the devil—for the heavenly reward of one more remission, and God, please let it last forever.

Despite familiarity with the beast, when the Great Depression of 1997 hit I was ill prepared. It attacked with the tenacity of a concrete-jungle trained pit bull, a dog placed on a treadmill with a kitten dangling just out of reach. Have you ever read about dogs like this, what they will do—run themselves into the ground—as they reach for their prey?

To my advantage, at least I'd suffered through enough prior bouts to recognize this thing for what it was. To my further advantage, I am mother to a child who makes every day, even the lowest day, worth living; worth saying once again, once again: *I will lick this thing.* And, sadly, ironically, to my advantage I have the "gift" of the memory of the friends who could not fight it anymore. They are in the ground now.

For the past two years, I'd have to estimate that I've spent at least half (seems like more) suffering some degree of depression. And I've spent many, many exhausting months fighting back now. Sometimes with a vengeance, other times like a child fighting sleep after waking up at six A.M. and running hard, hard, hard 'til damn near midnight.

There are days when I want to give up. Not suicide. But there is that fantasy that creeps in time and again: *So what if I don't get out of bed for a few days . . . weeks . . . months? If it worked for Brian Wilson . . .*

Factors of the kick-her-while-she's-down variety surface and exacerbate. For instance, there are those who say impulsiveness brought me to this latest bout. Choices poorly made. *It's all your fault* taunt the voices.

I argue back. *My fault? MY FAULT? Explain to me the tumor, then. Tell me why losing the one job that ever really paid was timed so well to coincide with the dead transmission. The other random acts of unkindness foisted upon me by the universe. Did I will these, too?*

None of this matters, really. The arguments are moot. What matters now is that I am standing here. The waters of depression are receding. But, as after any flood, there are many puddles to be mopped up. And, as with a flood, I need help, and help is always slower in coming as the need for it increases.

Along the lines of that analogy: Just as even those who love you most grow tired of coming over to help you move still more post-hurricane, water-logged furniture to the curb, get sick of hearing how your insurance coverage will not afford you the new floor you need to replace the warped one, so too do friends grow weary of hearing how depressed you are. They mean well, oh they do. But can they take one more moment of catharsis, another second of rehashing, the two hundredth report that yet another thing has gone wrong?

Often, they cannot. And so, far quicker than floodwater, all but the hardiest recede. Because they must. Deep inside your brain, relegated to the part that works perfectly well when there is no depression, you know they are not out to punish you. Nevertheless, it's still hard to avoid the deep end of self-pity when the troops pull out.

*Catch-22.* Because, in times like these, the most healing potion of all is catharsis. Which might be why therapists do brisk business when comradeship falls by the wayside. It is this same catharsis that drives others away. The phone rings less because no one wants to hear about the pain anymore. But if I cannot say it out loud, and say it a million times, how will I ever exorcise this thing from my soul?

The cycle spins in other directions. Isolation rules. You hide when you can. Either in your house alone or by hiding the thing eating you most. *Me? Oh I'm fine.*

I'm getting good at this, though. I am examining this condition in persons both first and third. My pain has built my compassion. I don't hate those who bailed, because I know they had to. They could not stick me back together. Because I am the one holding the glue gun here. This shattering effect, the broken pieces must ultimately be reconstructed by me.

As with physical therapy, the mental variety involves endless hours of going through the motions. In therapy I am a beginning swimmer, aquaphobic, a kickboard in my hands, a life vest on my chest. I am not swimming really, I am only pretending. But pretending is the only way to manage that first lap—how many times I have swum it now, tricked myself into believing I could long enough to cross the pool, flailing all the way?

And so I set out. Each morning I make my bed. A silly thing, perhaps, but always—regardless of all chaos around me—a single sign of orderliness I can retreat to. Retreat to without falling into and hiding beneath the covers because I'd hate to rumple them.

I take the vitamins. I walk miles daily, knowing somewhere in the recesses that, while the first step will be hard, by the thousandth the endorphins will deliver sweet relief. I force down lettuce and beans and rice. I shy from the temporary comfort of fat-laden, sleep-inducing options. I listen to music. In the car, I let the tears out in measured drops, allowing only the dog to play audience. I plant a garden.

At first, nothing grows. The ground remains dark and dry. The salad tastes like crap. The hike and bike trail seems endless. And loathsome. The dog looks confused.

In the mornings now, I wake the child up and pour his cereal. This is progress. A year ago it was so awful I could not do something so simple, relying heavily on the breakfast menu of the BK Lounge.

It is receding now. Daily we walk through the puddles together. After Cheerios, we go to the garden. Look, the corn is coming up. And the squash and the beans and the peas. In the afternoons we go to a field and he tests out his newfound bike-riding skills or lolls beside me on the blanket. He can read now. We can sit, engrossed in our respective books, apart yet connected.

I look at the shards at my feet. They are coming together now. Slowly. The picture they reflect back is far different than it once was. It is broken. But soon I will piece it together again, learn to accept this new image flashing altered back at me.

(1998)

## MS. B

Out driving, I hit scan, searching. Sweet and climbing like a honeysuckle vine, a Scottish lilt fills the car, achingly delivers the tale of "The Queen's Maries."

I sing along, poorly but enthusiastically. *There was Mary Beaton, and Mary Seaton, Mary Carmichael, and me . . .* It's a Celtic ballad I learned, sitting rapt, private concert, courtesy of my sixth-grade teacher.

Reason escapes, but I recall loathing Ms. B at first. She persisted nonetheless, revealing only decades later that we had been the worst class. Ever. That on top of our hell-raising, she'd been struggling with chronic knife-to-the-head migraines, a son so sick she spent many nights in ER. We never knew. But then, there was so much we did not know.

In a tiny town where ignorance equaled bliss, and blue-collared husbands came home to hot meals waiting, higher learning was not something one aspired to. Daddy as cartographer mapped out how it would be. Grow up. Get a job. Get a husband. Have babies. Stay in the right lane.

But I was a hungry girl. Eager. Defiant. Swallowing books whole, always wanting to know more more more. Swimming in a sea of nine siblings, I thrashed, reaching for the buoyancy of attention. *Someone look at me, please. Tell me what else there is.*

She saw my hand, desperate, waving: *Pick me, pick me!* She did. Fed the hunger. Copied big my poetry, displaying it for all to see. I can still see it hanging there. Red construction paper frame. *I believe in you* written between all the lines.

After school, she taught me, too. The chords—G, C, D, E minor. The words—Peter, Paul and Mary, Joan Baez, Bob Dylan. The answer, her steady voice assured me, was blowing in the wind.

The wind blew me, hard, when I fled at eighteen. But some radio in some town along the way would deliver one of those old tunes, return her to me.

News came of her son's death. I wrote to her then, knowing even before I was a mother myself there are no words to console one who outlives her child. That was so long ago. And then we lost touch.

Last winter I went back to the place now behind me half a lifetime. In my mother's kitchen I eat white squares of American cheese sliced thin—no thinner than that—straight from the butcher paper. Nieces and nephews fill a Sunday morning. Cousin cacophony.

My brother's daughter Jess announces her teacher for the year.

I light up. *Ms. B was my favorite!* I tell her. I scrawl a hello and my address on a scrap of paper for Jess to pass on.

A month later, twenty-five years since first we met, I tear open the note bearing her return address. I write back, enclose some of my writing, even the unsettling stuff, things that happened that she never knew. I tell her I don't want to make her sad. But I do want her to see what I've accomplished. Even now I want to make her proud.

In her response she mentions other kids in my class, the hell they went through at home. Their long forgotten faces return, vivid. I never knew.

She reminds me what I wrote when she lost her son. *You taught me to think,* I told her. True. Strong woman, bell-clear voice, delivering anthems of freedom, urging me to seek my own.

Revolution. Spin. Circle around. Return to the place that you were.

She was a center to my universe then. I always loved the part where I set down my twenty dollar guitar, sat back, watched her fingers fly over twelve strings, felt that voice bounce off the chalkboard, vibrate to my core.

She was going to quit teaching she said. Because he died. My letter helped her stick it out. It was a tiny gift compared to what she'd given me. The things she still gives to kids like Jess (whom, she tells me, asks as many questions as someone else she knows.)

I drive through life, scanning thoughts I'd rather not think. Search for a stopping place. Her voice comes through and I pause to listen. Songs of revolution. Words of hope. (2001)


## SUMMER

It's coming. Though the windows are closed on this odd-chilly late spring day in Texas, still, I can smell it out there, imminent. The calendar suggests its official arrival as sometime late in June. I know better.

In no time, it will be here, made official not by solstice but by school year's final bell.

Summer.

I love it.

Summer is the season I've had the biggest crush on since before I was born. I'm certain that floating in my own little amniotic ocean prompted this lifetime love of mine. For first and foremost, I associate summer with the salty sea, specifically the Atlantic, where I spent my first twenty summers, where I still return whenever I can.

My summer love is more complicated than mere enveloping heat and cooling water, though. This fixation of mine, examined, broken down into components, scrutinized for some core, yields only an answer about as tangible as a bay breeze.

I cannot put my finger upon the source of this love, but it is True Love and I can see that nostalgia plays an enormous role. Such roots confessed, I hastily note I am hardly ashamed of the role sentiment plays when it comes to these deep fond feelings I forever hold for Summer, my love, as I recall our many cherished moments together.

Perhaps rumination upon personal history is the tool to shed light upon my adoration of soaring temperatures, scorched and peeling red skin, lethargy across the boards of beast and man alike.

Beyond early amniotic imprint—*warmth and salt water good!*—came another lesson in summer's supremacy early on in life. After nearly six years of being glued to my mother's side without interruption from the outside world, suddenly I was wrenched away to school, replete with its schedules and demands: freedom stolen.

Freedom restored came but once a year: Summer, of course.

Summer when, even if daily there was a pile of mom-issued chores, deadlines for completion were looser and, these deadlines met, the day then stretched out long and full of the promise of everything or nothing at all.

How can they teach us, from kindergarten through bachelor's degree (or longer) that summers are life's designated respite, only to have this privilege ripped from us come true adulthood's cruelty: Real Jobs?

Is it any wonder so many people hate working, what with it meaning an end to the three-month annual break they'd grown so used to? Is it a surprise that many schoolteachers will flat out tell you that, more than any love of kids, it's *summers off* that keeps them coming back to deal with a new crop of smartass students and cranky parents each fall?

My parents built a beach house around the time I was born.

Nothing fancy. A big square Sheetrock box. A mile or so from the beach. No heating. No a/c. Beds, many of them, in every room, including the kitchens (upstairs and down).

These (the kitchens, the beds) occurred in multiples to accommodate the renters we had to have many seasons in order to afford keeping the place. And to accommodate us nine kids. And later to accommodate various clusters of *our* two dozen kids. It is a house they sold after nearly forty years and amidst great cries of collective anguish.

There was nothing magic you could touch in the furniture that mostly was curbside castoff, the cheap linoleum floors, the fake paneling that eventually covered the graffiti that originally covered the Sheetrock. The magic was inherent to, more than anything else, a time of year and all it represented.

Summer.

In my childhood we went there summer weekends plus two weeks in August, so we could be there for the Feast of the Assumption when, they say, the water is blessed to commemorate the rising into heaven of the Virgin Mary, body and all. When the life guards row a priest out upon the waves and every Catholic from a three-state radius comes walking or crawling or carried in wheelchairs out to water's edge, to be cured by this holy water.

Summer was my cousins Johnny and Theresa coming to visit our Mom-mom, with her own summerhouse near ours. Johnny teaching then beating me at chess, summer nights. Theresa, a couple years my senior, whispering to me rumors about some kind of kissing they do in France, as we speculated about cute boys from renter families across the street, never to be seen again after this week, looking so hot riding their bikes into that chemical fog shooting off the back of the mosquito truck.

Times we weren't at the beach house down the shore, I found the magic anyway. Sneaking next door to my best friend's house, watching verboten soap operas while gorging on snacks that always seemed better than at home. Surprised and relieved that, despite nine months of not watching, the plots and characters were all just about exactly the same.

Summers were books, checked out of a small-town library or culled, dusty and musty, from a curious collection passed down by some great uncle in publishing who died before I was born.

I'd escape in these pages, off on adventures with Trixie Beldon, girl sleuth, or Nancy Drew, other girl sleuth, or the Happy Hollisters, a whole family of child sleuths. The March sisters, those Little Women, were my best summer companions though, especially feisty Jo, validating that to be defiant was never easy but always, always worth it.

Summers changed as I got older. Buckets and shovels on the beach traded in for *Seventeen* magazines and baby oil (better to baste you as you lie, frying, melanoma not yet a word in the common vocabulary). Then teenage summer grunt jobs—boardwalk gigs and chamber-maiding and waitressing stints, no longer tourist but now servant to them.

Still, the magic stayed.

I've lived landlocked now for a good fifteen years—who can say why? (I certainly can't.) As such, it is often necessary for me to substitute some river or lake for summer's requisite liquid component, settling as a lover of salted-margaritas sometimes must when the bartender runs out of salt.

If really pressed, I will lie prone on my towel by the neighborhood concrete pond and—with relentless sun pounding down upon closed eyelids—conjure a fantasy crystal-ocean-and-pristine-sand paradise from the reality of kiddie-pee and chlorine-enhanced six-foot-deep puddle beside me.

Still, I can return to the magic regardless of circumstance, and I do, often, knocking off early from my work, lolling about, indulging in gossipy magazines with nothing of substance or lasting value to offer, continuing to seek out a deep tan (never mind the warnings not to).

And though my own child has not ever lived near the ocean, I first took him there at six months, with more than a few return trips in the ten summers since. I give him other summer rituals, too. Summer camps, road trips to see his dad and aunts and uncles and cousins. Bike rides to the pool. Afternoon matinees, where the a/c is so much better and cheaper than running our old big window unit that forever sounds like some 747 about to take off in the living room.

It is coming. Soon. We can smell it. And we are waiting. For that bell ending school. Starting summer.                    (2002)

Back in 1989, heart full, pockets empty, tired of long-distance love, I moved to St. Louis to be with my man. A need for quick work led me to a restaurant called Riddle's Penultimate.

It was one of those jobs where you can't help thinking as the years pass and the coworker friendships deepen—though you all moved on long ago—that some force greater than the quest for tips pulled you into the joint in the first place. I left less than a year later, but never lost touch with my fellow waitresses Doris, Megan, and Sue.

Doris was thirty-seven then, and from a background so rough she made the rest of our childhood experiences seem like Disney World on a short-line day. Back when she was little, you had to beat your kid pretty bad for it to make the paper. Doris's dad made the paper.

But Doris had a spark. Despite the dark shadow her father cast and the attendant adult pain and bad choices the darkness often prompted, she maintained hope, carrying on when a lot of people would've checked out. I have a permanently etched mind-flash of her zipping through Riddle's while I think: *When I turn thirty-seven it will be my best year ever.*

I have no idea why that thought seized me right then, but it never left. I waited a dozen years, often impatient, for thirty-seven to arrive, sure that with it would come some amazing something.

I just turned thirty-eight. Instant retrospect suggests thirty-seven to have been, at best, an odd mix with more than a few bumps and backslides than I was bargaining for when I stood longingly on the cusp of eager expectation.

But yet, like Doris, despite the regular appearance of dark clouds, I remain hopeful, sometimes to my own surprise. Recently, joking in email with my physics friend Tom, whom I was consulting for guidance to help the kid with math homework, I asked this peripheral question: What is the lowest common multiplier of stupidity and hope?

*Faith* came the immediate response.

I especially like it when science types toss around this concept. I need all the reminders I can get. Faith. The driving force. I wear a mustard seed around my neck. Don't talk to me about religion. I'm not interested. Faith though. That's a good one. The mustard seed came from my friend, Serena, eighty-seven, who like Doris has seen more sorrows in one lifetime than any one person should have to bear.

Looking past the obstacles encountered, I have to admit the little messages and rewards brought to me in year thirty-seven were abundant. Among them:

- Frequent flyer miles and generous friends help my son and me pull off a trip to Japan despite severe budgetary constraints. All we see and feel and eat fills us, changing our perspective forever. Returning, one vision revisits most: At a temple at sunset, clouds part, revealing distant Mount Fuji.

- Discussing with Henry the difference between empathy and sympathy: I say, if you see a guy with a broken leg and you have broken your leg you know his pain, so that's empathy. Sympathy, I say, is if you haven't broken your leg but you still feel bad.

  During this chat, we pass a man with leopard-print-dyed hair which, how about that, Henry also happens to have. I point at the man's hair and ask, "Empathy?" "No," says my son, "because that is not pain. That is beauty!"

- I fall in love. With mopping. Not for purposes of cleanliness. (Actually, I mop around stuff.) I just like the smell of the Pine Sol, the instant gratification of a momentarily unmuddy floor. And I like it because, as with cooking, mopping reminds me to play music, loud.

- A few days after September 11th, my friend Amy makes it back to Austin. She was on the runway at National in DC when the Pentagon was hit. Her best friend died on Flight 11. Amy is shaken. Six of us walk together, seeking comfort.

Amy is tiny with bright blonde hair. As we walk and talk suddenly she begins jumping and clapping, racing forward into the arms of a man we soon learn is her twin brother's best friend. The man is huge and black and lifting Amy off the ground. When he sets her down, we notice a smaller olive-ish guy—Middle Eastern perhaps?— clinging to the big man's side, nearly obscured by his girth.

The small man, a total stranger, exclaims, "I just wanted to be part of all the love!" and jogs off.

• At the bakery near my house, I stop one very cold night to get Henry a hot chocolate. The counter guy flashes a grin, says he's buying. I protest (my default setting: give, never take) only to be firmly instructed, "Sometimes, you just have to let the universe give you stuff."

• I spend the last day of 2001 walking alone through Missouri Botanical Garden. It's about eighteen degrees. It is barren and icy and the koi in the Japanese Garden are far below the water, not surfacing to fight for food like in summer.

I am back in St. Louis thinking about a lot of things. It is a nostalgic place for me. It is where my son's father still lives. He is eight months sober now, sober for the first time in over twenty years. Henry and I are amazed, thankful . . . nervous. Even good change takes adjusting.

I end my walk at the Linnean House, warm and bursting with blooms, where I meditate, which I have not done since that day in September when faith wavered, concentration blew away.

I start the new year as I ended the old, returning to the gardens the next day. My old friends Megan and Sue join me. Sue takes us to a fountain, now dry, where last summer she brought her dad, broke the rules by letting him dunk his feet in moving water—a final wish before his decision to stop dialysis ended this life for him eight decades after it began.

• On my neighborhood walk one day, a picture smaller than these materializes. Smaller but bigger, too, and just as permanent. A Mercedes is driving toward me and I am trying to figure out what the driver is doing. She pulls by the side of the road and I feel irritation, projecting upon her a stereotype for what she's driving and how she looks.

She gets out of the car, walks past me up the road. I turn, watch. She approaches the fresh-killed body of a squirrel, prone and bloody in the middle of the street. She reaches down gingerly, lifts his body, cradles him, carries him to more sacred ground, lays him down. A little dignity for the dead.

I choke up, wave. *Thank you,* I say. *For more reasons than I can name.* (2002)

TO HAVE AND HAVE NOT
(WORK/MONEY)

People ask me how I came to be a professional writer. In my case, I realized early on that you could get money for your words. In fact, my very first submission netted me a $25 savings bond, an event for which I still suffer the delusion that everything I write will sell, first draft, every time.

In the case of that first essay, I was a fifth grader in Ignorance, New Jersey. I won second place for a piece I wrote, the precise topic of which escapes me now, but I know it was something like: *Why I Love Firemen* or *Firemen Are Great* or *Give Me a Man in Red Suspenders and I Will Live Forever.*

Inspired more, I admit, by the money than the honor, I went on to enter and win a number of other essay competitions. Again, precise themes elude me, but based on the year ('76) and the political sentiment of the town, here are some safe and logical guesses: *Wow! The Bicentennial, COOL!; Why I Love Our Flag!; Education Is Swell!; We Need Peace on This Earth NOW!; When I Grow Up, I Want to Be a Nurse or a Nun so I Can Help Lots of People and Get into Heaven, Too!*

Though I didn't realize it at the time, those exclamation-point ridden pieces were excellent training for the grown up writer I would become. In particular, they gave me the foundation I needed to go on to write for glossy women's magazines. Such pieces as *Why I'll Never Marry!; Single Mom Half Dead but Happy!; Getting Used to Being Thin!;* and, of course, *Give Me a Man in Red Suspenders and I Will Live Forever!*

But life wasn't all essays and the glossies were two decades away. To kill time and practice form, I toyed with fiction on the side.

My first novel (if you don't include the one I wrote in fourth grade about a talking saxophone, and please, don't include that one), was written at the height of my prepubescent angst, and, shockingly enough, centered on an unhappy, angst-ridden, prepubescent girl who loved milkshakes and boys, though she had far more success in procuring the former.

Finally, after endless lonely days, and empty nights filled with longing, she finds a boy who likes her back. One day, she and the boy are at a park not unlike the one at the end of my real-life street. He is pushing her—higher, higher, higher—and she is giddy with the rush of the swing and the pounding of her heart. Until . . . the horrible accident. Thud. She falls from the swing, leading not to a simple concussion but rather a shattering that drives a splinter of bone straight into her gray matter.

Does she die? Of course. But not right away. First, she is given six months to live by the doctors. This is cause for a poignant second half of the novel, in which our protagonist reflects upon not only her ongoing pre-pube angst, but the pain of dying young and in love.

When I showed this, or discussed it anyway, with my best friend (who not surprisingly would grow up to become a nurse), she chastised me, particularly for the entry in which the young girl laments, "Well, only three days left to live!"

Beth pointed out that the six-month prognosis would have had to have been an approximation. Then she laughed in my face. It was my first experience with literary criticism. I think I shunned her for a week. I also scrapped the project.

But, as proof that writers are born not made, I again soon found myself unable to keep away from plotting. I fashioned a short story—the first I ever submitted for publication—about an angst-ridden post-pubescent young woman who finally meets a man who likes her. They fall deeply in love and make hasty preparations to wed, only to discover on the eve of their ill-fated pairing that somehow (and forgive me for forgetting my clever literary device) they can never consummate, never feel joy again even, because, as it turns out, *THEY ARE ACTUALLY LONG-LOST BROTHER AND SISTER!!* The piece was promptly rejected by that pinnacle of the fiction world—*Teen* magazine.

Here, I'd like to stop for a moment and delve into rejection, the greatest sacrament in the high order of writing. Rejection is funny. It makes you want to puke. It also drives you to "prove to those jerks how stupid they were for not publishing my story about the angst-ridden woman who practically marries her brother."

I already was well versed in rejection, thanks to my father, long before I could hold a pencil. In fact, I think the day I received that first rejection letter, I felt an odd sense of relief: Should my father suddenly fall off a swing and get a brain splinter and, after six months, die, there was a whole world of surrogates just waiting to put me down, tell me no, give me that negative feedback I had come to expect.

Yes, but how did I wind up as a professional? The answer lies in a crazy man I met in a hotel room in Ocean City, New Jersey, when I was nineteen years old. George convinced me to let him shave off the bulk of my Breck-girl hair. When I returned to college, a month later, I made the stark discovery that girls with flattops were not all the rage in Central Florida, circa 1983.

Ah, but the silver lining. Fortunately for me, a group of passing frat boys insulted me to just the proper boiling point necessary to prompt a letter to the editor of the school paper detailing how girls with flattops have feelings too, and how would you like it if someone made fun of you, and by the way, screw the dingdang Sig-Eps.

The paper ran this letter as a guest column, which changed my life forever. Soon, I was made cub reporter and sent on dangerous, undercover assignments. Well, one dangerous, undercover assignment. I tried out for the Sun Dolls, a troupe of athletic supporter dancing girls not talented enough to be cheerleaders. For five days I step-ball-changed to the right and back while the rest of the group surged left and front. I didn't make the team, but the five-part exposé was the break I had been waiting for. I wasn't just a writer—I was a star, gosh darn it. And I was making four dollars an hour, too.

Things started really cooking then. I got a weekly column. I extolled on life's mysteries great and small. I bashed frats whenever possible and when that got boring, I lashed out elsewhere. An account of my first trip to the gynecologist— replete with tales of sea monkeys swimming in my cha-cha—really wowed 'em.

And then there was that little pope-bashing parable where an innocent but disillusioned young lass goes to confession, laments every aspect of the church, demands to know if only men get to be priests because all knowledge is stored in the penis, and then, those things unburdened from her bosom, she shoots off the priest's kneecaps.

For some reason, this pope-piece seemed to offend the campus

Catholics. And the city Catholics. And the fifty-seven sundry Catholics who called from all over the state demanding I be crucified.

In response, my editors tightened the leash until finally I quit. But not to worry, for just around the corner, waiting to be impressed by my collected writings, were the editors at Whittle Communications in Knoxville, Tennessee. They offered an internship and I jumped on it. Forget Tampa, I thought. I shall shine in Knoxville.

Shine I did. As the tireless and ever cheerful intern of *Veterinary Practice Management Magazine*, I wrote endless masterpieces. How to put your dog on a diet. What vets do in their spare time. How to give accurate directions to your office (*Make a right at the fire hydrant, ho ho!*), and, naturally, a series on pit bull aggression read by dozens of vets everywhere.

But something was missing in my life. I started to realize what so many other girls—even my own protagonists of days gone by—already knew: success was okay, but the real reason we're on this earth is to make men like us. So I did what I had to do. I found one. He lived in St. Louis. I packed up my '77 Aspen wagon with the slant six engine and headed west to the city that is home to that literary lion, *St. Louis Magazine.*

They were much impressed by my deft Sun Doll and pit bull reports, and sent me on yet another investigative adventure. I visited every weight loss clinic in the city, feigning serious interest in paying thousands of dollars to let minimum wage workers in deceptively professional looking white lab jackets show me how to lose weight by eating three-dimensional pictures of food.

Though that was a cover story (my first), and a good-sized piece, I was still a small-time writer, augmenting the hundreds of dollars I earned annually through my writing with sundry foodservice jobs. Then one day, the call of a lifetime came.

A PR firm in New York needed a writer to rewrite the age-old booklet given to angst-ridden prepubescent girls, gently coaxing them into womanhood while simultaneously, though subtly, reminding them if they didn't use Crampax brand tampons, they would burn in hell. Worse, boys wouldn't like them. Would four thousand dollars be enough?

*Hell yes,* I shouted. *I love Crampax Tampons! I think I'll start wearing them every day!*

My friend Mike suggested I title this epic, *So, You Wanna Wear a White Bikini?* I liked it, but unfortunately the PR firm was insistent we choose something that in no way would even vaguely refer to the booklet's contents.

Ultimately, we settled on *Days of Wonder,* as in: *I wonder when someone is going to tell me what the hell really is going on down there.*

Certainly the sponsors were hell-bent against dispensing such information—they made me keep things as gray as possible. I could say, for example, *Expect to grow hair in places you never had it before.* I could not say if this meant the bottom of your feet or under your fingernails.

And under no circumstances was I to mention the potential of getting knocked up. Odd, not just for the obvious reasons, but you would think the tampon folks would want to prevent as many pregnancies as possible thereby insuring more monthly shedding and, consequently, greater use of their product.

I didn't waste much time worrying about what role I might be playing in impregnating fifth graders, though. That check came in and I had better things to think about. Now that I was a mother, and beginning to settle down, I needed to find a new city where I knew no one, a place to hurl myself back into chaos.

I chose Austin, Texas, the city where at last I would become a full-time writer. Of term papers.

Allow me to quote myself (a favorite pastime) from a piece *Texas Monthly* would eventually publish, detailing this short-lived career:

> The paper that most tried my creative skills was an analysis of how growing up Jewish in a gentile community had affected my life. Having grown up in a solid Irish-Catholic neighborhood, I took on the paper as a test of my true aspiration to become an award-winning fiction writer. I called upon my memory to recount all the Jewish-experience books I'd ever read. I took myself back to seventh grade, when I attended my friend Erica's bas mitzvah. I contended that it had not been easy, but that I had learned many valuable lessons. I got a B-plus. Ironically, the same grade I'd received on a real autobiography I'd written years before, in eighth grade.
>
> I realized that I had become a sort of expert—not in any

subject, but in college-speak. I could create what appeared to be a well-thought out piece on almost any topic. Let's say I wanted to analyze my son's favorite book, Dr. Seuss's *Hop on Pop*. I could present seven surefire papers on this masterpiece: Christian influence (the image of three fish in a tree and its relevance to the Trinity); sexual ethics (Mr. Brown eating suspiciously phallic snacks, leaves his wife to cavort with Mr. Black); death imagery (Is Mr. Black actually a dark symbol of death that befalls those seeking unconventional sex?); sexism (Why do the brothers and father read while mother stands by mute?); racism (Mr. Brown and Mr. Black as indicators of interracial relationships); philosophical pondering (When Will goes uphill, does the hill become his property? Would Locke argue that this path leads away from happiness?); and, finally, good versus evil (The children claim it is fun to hop on Pop. Pop says, "Stop, you must not hop on Pop?" Who is right?). These thoughts, sandwiched between opening and closing paragraphs that say exactly the same thing in slightly altered ways, would, I guarantee, net me at least a C, often a B.

After about four months of the academy, I'd had more than enough. I cut back on writing papers and took on a restaurant job to make ends meet. Soon, slinging hash took precedence over slinging bull.

It would take some time before my fingers again ventured away from the cash register and back—little writing addicts that they are—to the keyboard. (1996)

## HERE, KITTY, KITTY

Never mind the six dead guinea pigs buried in my backyard. That was just due to one of those *sure-we-can-get-rodents* parental forays into grave misjudgment—the sort of experiment that invariably leads to A Child's First Lesson in the Rapid Reproductive Cycle and Too-Short Life Span of Small Furry Things. Really, I'm pretty good with animals.

Good enough, in fact, that when others get truly desperate due to some unforeseen no-room-at-the-kennel pre-vacation crisis, I am called upon to guard their precious pets. For instance, I considered it nothing but a fun challenge the time ten of thirteen cats I was watching (yes, in the same house) caught colds and needed to be force-fed their little kitty cold pills.

I found it downright hilarious that three pairs among this bunch resembled each other so closely that I never could quite keep track if I'd under-dosed one while overdosing another. Besides, I was distracted from the guilt that I'd maybe screwed up by all those endearing little claws proving, yes, heavy denim can be penetrated by teeny feline switchblades.

One day, while tending these very cats, the high jinks reached critical mass when, hazarding a glance in the toilet I spotted . . .

A snake.

Okay, so it was a small snake. And dead. Still—for a good while after that incident, I had a real hard time using the facilities (any facilities), for fear of having my batonkis swallowed whole by an urban, pipe-dwelling anaconda.

The snake-in-the-toilet pales by comparison to the one-hundred-pound "puppies" left in my care by the Pathological Yuppie Liar Couple. Though mutts, you could clearly see their bloodline—half Hounds from Hell, half Scooby Doo on crack.

I should've suspected during our preliminary appointment—the pooches were on choke chains *inside* the house—that things weren't exactly Lassie laid-back here. But Dick and Jane assured me their "babies" were well trained.

A few nights later, Dick dropped them off, along with ninety-five previously undiscussed "necessities," from Bourgeoisie Brand dog food to security blankies to eye medication to the tether that Hailey must stay on because—oops, did he forget to mention this?—"She's a real Houdini!" Thankfully, Dick did stop short of demanding that I pre-masticate the kibble.

When the "housebroken" "puppies" let fly all manner of excrement throughout my house (*and* destroyed the gifts under the tree) even I, Miss Find Humor in Most Everything, stopped laughing. For days I futilely tried to reach Dick and Jane at their emergency numbers. (I did reach Dick's irritated mother who, hearing the alarm in my voice, said, exasperated, as if this might console me, *Well doesn't it just figure—two communication majors and they can't keep in touch.*) When at last I did track them down, I announced the dogs would be going back home.

"You can't do that," Dick protested. "They'll wreck the place!"

That was Christmas Eve. Christmas morning, six A.M., while other kids were tiptoeing into their living rooms to see what the obese elf had left, my kid, shivering and groggy in the car, was hurtling with me toward doggie hell to feed the beasts and verify Dick's prognostication skills.

A gift awaited us. Bile-covered pieces of my dog's favorite chew toy, the (formerly) happy-faced rubber carrot, which the hell hounds had apparently eaten along with half of my other possessions. Big surprise—the couple shorted me a considerable portion of my fee upon their return, citing that we never had nailed down a solid figure and I had failed to keep the dogs at my house.

There have been smaller disasters, nerve-wracking nonetheless. One client left his a/c off in August. The heat cooked his fish. Not having the courtesy to perform a synchronized death ritual, the school left me perpetually anxious. Each day, driving toward the house, I'd suffer a severe case of Hitchcockian Gut Disorder, stomach clenched with anxiety and bowels trembling in suspense: *Which would be next?*

(One reader, upon hearing this, wrote to tell me of a friend who'd suffered similar circumstances. Day one of a fish-sitting gig, they'd all up and died. He retrieved them from the tank and stuck them in the freezer. The day before the owner returned, he took the frozen fish to the pet store, slapped them up on the counter, and instructed the staff, "Match 'em." The owner never knew the difference. I'm pretty sure this method won't work with dogs.)

Then there was Thanksgiving with Emma, the purebred Labrador with four-foot vertical leap and bionic-butt-wiggle action skills. I'm positive that when God was handing out Labrador brains, Emma was in the other room eating her own barf. Emma, miraculously, only knocked me down once. To her credit, she is in full control of her gastrointestinal system.

Pip the Rat Terrier is a favorite. Four pounds of trembling I-Want-To-Snuggle-In-Your-Lap-At-All-Times eagerness, Pip's perpetual manifestation of her excitability is her trademark Excitement Pee. (Not to be confused with the displays of enthusiasm

**57**

offered by Bruno the Amorous Dachshund who, à la Pepe Le Pew, will attempt to hump everything from my ankle to my fuzzy study pillow, twenty-four hours a day. Or Judo, the cockatiel, who whistles "The Girl from Ipanema.")

Down south of the river reside a half-dozen cats, doted upon by their humans, who named them all for brands of booze except The Kitten (weighing in at about twenty pounds). The humans attached to these felines have extremely high standards for their darlings. I am paid handsomely to visit twice daily, to sprinkle upon carefully measured scoops of dry food (diet for The Kitten) a garlic powder cat health supplement. The indoor cats must not go out. The outdoor cats must not go in. I am to send daily updates via their pager, which I do. ("All Purrrrfect!")

The only real problem I have with these folks is that something about their house turns me flat out stupid. Like that time when, delighted to have just purchased my first ever car without an oil leak, I celebrated by parking in the driveway, secure in the knowledge I wouldn't leave a nasty stain.

Running around front to retrieve the mail, I heard a crash and chalked it up to rowdy neighbors. Only when I noticed my car wasn't where I left it did I realize I'd neglected to engage the emergency brake. The damage to the garage was negligible (the noise courtesy of a toppled bicycle within). But the panic induced was palpable.

It's the hardest part of pet sitting. Being responsible for other people's stuff and, more importantly, their beloved beasts is stress-inducing to say the least.

Which is why, when all the humans return, it's my turn. I take their money, hop in my oil-leak-free car and run. Far away. For a little break.

Of course I leave enormous bowls of food and water for my own animals. I'm sure they enjoy their time alone.          (2000)


## BROKE.COM

Last year was a financial anomaly in my life. I made a killing, living joyously and lavishly off the Fat of the Land.com as I created Web "content," often commanding ludicrously enormous fees in the process. For a while, as did many of my peers in this Fantasy.com, I even sported a spectacular title: "Producer"— for an Oprah Winfrey–approved-and-backed Web site, no less. *Woo-woo!*

Even after I left that full-time gig and returned to life as a Web freelancer, I continued to haul in the cash.

It was great, like one of those teen movies where the parents go out of town for the weekend and leave their platinum credit cards behind, in plain sight. The venture capitalists dumped millions into the start-ups. The start-ups heaped money on the content-producing contractors formerly known as starving writers. We "content specialists," in turn, thrilled at the jump in income, hurled our money everywhere (as did everyone else in the industry).

Personally, I went nuts. Not as nuts as some . . . I didn't take exotic vacations to bond with elephants at the foot of Mt. Kilimanjaro (though I enjoyed a long weekend in San Francisco). I didn't buy a million-dollar loft downtown (though I was able to stay in my rental house despite the boomtown rent increase and the fact that some selfish dot jackass contacted my landlady—the house wasn't for sale—and offered her about four times what it's actually worth. God bless the landlady; she said no.) I didn't purchase a Porsche Boxter (though I did score a thirteen hundred dollar '85 Subaru, my youngest vehicle yet, with a mere 125,000 on the odometer). And I didn't build up my portfolio (actually, I don't *have* a portfolio—but I did pay off a substantial amount of credit card debt "acquired" during previous, drier years as a writer).

For me, extravagance equaled other things: Getting a Chango's Mahi-Mahi burrito whenever the hell I wanted one, handing out wads of cash to my strapped friends ("Here, keep it!"), overcompensating my kid for all the years I had to say, "Sorry honey, we can't, we're broke." Oh, and I bought toilet paper—my favorite name brand—in bulk.

Yep, I was out of control.

It was great. And now, as Jesus said on the cross, "It is finished." The parents are home, so to speak. The dot-coms are dead.

As the story goes, Jesus lived again. So, too, might some mutation of the Internet resurrect as a place of ample and profitable work. For now, though, Austin is unemployment city for so many of us who, just months ago, had some of the best salaries in town.

Not officially employed by one company, I cannot be officially laid off. Not laid off, I cannot collect unemployment. Nor do I have a severance package to fall back on. Or a trust fund. (Nor worthless dot-stocks upon which to heap false hope for overnight millionairedom, only to discover—as have many—that one's morning crap is currently worth more, so much more, than those hundred thousand shares in Godwewerestupidweren'twe.com.)

Regardless, I am broke. Totally. Didn't save a dime. Suspended my disbelief as I always do those rare times the money flows. Nope, I sent my cash packing hard and fast.

Back to square one, starving artist land, I keep waiting to freak out, to panic. There is, in the back of my mind, a little pestering voice: "Earth to Spike: We have a child and five animals to feed, and the gas bill was fifteen thousand dollars last month!" But after a year glued to my computer, of going damn near blind working crazy hours, panic now, curiously, remains at bay. Mostly I'm in happy awe.

Granted, knowledge that those few straggly checks from past work will be showing up briefly aids in my calm. Plus I always have some little writing assignment or two floating around, some pet-sitting gig, some odd job. If I budget, I can stretch this money.

It's an abrupt adjustment—going from a year where it was not at all uncommon to earn six thousand dollars per month, to a year where less than 2K monthly is the average, with fully half earmarked for the landlady. Call me twisted, but I enjoy the challenge. You know—man vs. nature, man vs. man, woman vs. empty bank account.

Forced to cut back, I have looked around at what is unnecessary and, no matter how much I love it, I have eradicated it. No more YMCA membership. No more after-school care. No more smoking. Admittedly, quitting is something I did for my health, but there's no denying it saves more than a thousand bucks a year.

Lucky for me, broke feels familiar. I grew up and spent most of my adult life in the vicinity of poor. If you've spent any time at all as a have-not, you understand. There is resourcefulness and creativity to making ends meet. A mouthful of happiness recalling how much you actually do love rice and beans and that Martha White cornbread mix that costs, like, thirty cents a package.

At the risk of irreversible bad instant karma, I admit additional pleasure at the dot-com demise, derived from knowing certain someones are suffering. One guy in particular comes to mind. Last summer, writing for the *New York Times Magazine*, Helen Thorpe set out to capture the "new Austin"—the boomtown economy, high-tech glitz, yadda yadda. One quote haunts me still.

As Thorpe reported: "Earlier this year, at a gathering of local software CEOs called the Austin 360 Summit . . . Mayor [Kirk] Watson delivered an impassioned speech about the challenges facing the city. While the mayor was talking, a baby-faced CEO raised his hand 'Why are you looking at us to help with these community issues?' asked the software CEO. 'That's your job.'"

I hope that guy is down to his last three hundred dollar unemployment check. I hope he can't afford gas for his stupid SUV. I hope he's so disconnected from the community that he was so uninterested in that he's gone back from whence he came (pity those on his receiving end). And when he gets there, I hope he has to sling hash for a while, like in that Bob Wiseman song: *In her dreams, it's a big greasy spoon . . . and the doctors are finally waiters.* (Note poetic license allows substitution of "dot-commers" for doctors in this instance.)

For me, perhaps the very biggest thrill in all of this recession madness is precisely *community*—my personal community and heightened awareness of their ever-supportive ways.

More than once, I've needed a little help with the rent when the big contracts dried up. Help was right there. Dinner invites, already ample, seem to be on the upswing. Or maybe it's just that we have more time now to accept the generosity of food and the enormous pleasure of good company.

On the give side of the coin, I've used my new spare time to cook more for whoever cares to stop by. And I've bumped up my volunteer work. The payback on these activities is immediate. Interacting with others—something I had little time for when I was busting ass last year, eye on the golden ring—now helps me keep my head on straight while I regroup and come up with a new plan.

That new plan, for now, is to forgo seeking a forty-hour-per-week gig and stay at this lower income. Don't get me wrong—I had a swell time with all that money. It would be real nice to have it again. But I got a taste of being able to afford whatever, and I buried myself under a heap of what-doesn't-really-matter in the process. I, for one, am grateful to the current economic slump for shaking me up a little.

I'm going back to a little of this and a little of that. I'll be un-retiring my apron and signing up for a part-time food service gig, generously offered by a member of my *community*. What time I do have to write, I will spend writing what really counts and not writing—as I swear I did for one Web site—instructions telling women how to buy pants. For their *husbands*. ("Be sure to measure the waist *and* inseam.")

And if I should waver from this plan, start to contemplate big money, insane hours, and promises of the next great new economy, someone please stop me. Remind me to visualize that picture, the real-life one from last summer:

> I'm driving my kid to a friend's house. It's a fourteen-mile round-trip—used to take me thirty minutes, tops. That night, over an hour into it, sitting in more traffic still, I ob-serve yet another limousine pass me by as I look up at cranes blocking the stars. No shit—just then Pink Floyd chimed in on the radio:
> > *Money! It's a hit*
> > Don't give me that do goody good bullshit . . .

(2001)

## CALENDAR GIRL

I sat, staring into her eyes, trying to come up with words to cap-ture her. Occasionally, I'd glance down, take in her entire being. But the truth was, I preferred her eyes. Not so much for their dewy, limpid, bottomless-well qualities. But because focusing on her eyes meant I didn't have to focus on other facts.

Like that she was as close to being naked as you can be with-out actually being naked. Like that she was sporting a belt buckle the size of a trashcan lid that made her look entirely stupid.

Meet the cover girl from the *Caliente Calendar.*

It was my job one summer to describe her and her ilk at a com-pany that boasted selling the biggest collection of calendars in the universe. They'd just opened an online store and somebody needed to fill in product descriptions. That somebody was me.

Besides scantily clad babes—and, this being an equal world, lots of scantily clad dudes, too—I also had the pleasure of describing over two thousand other types of calendars. There were sports calendars, ferret calendars, tractor calendars, outdoors calendars, exotic destination calendars, cartoon calendars, car calendars, train calendars, famous artist calendars, schlock artist calendars, dog calendars, and cat calendars.

When one's job is describing calendars, one can become cynical rather quickly. One can joke, sardonically, that one can simply type into the catalogue database the same thing over and over again, à la Jack Nicholson's character in *The Shining*.

*This calendar has 365 days! A guaranteed four weeks per month! Lots of pictures! A dozen months!*

But then one would get fired. And one would not be able to meet one's landlord's needs. And one would thus be sad. And forced to get in touch with one's sadness while living on one's friend's couch.

And so, I did what I had to to keep my landlord doing the happy landlord dance of joy. Day after painfully-dragged-out-dreadfully-boring-make-you-want-to-scream-if-you-have-to-look-at-one-more-calendar day I worked toward my ultimate goal of finding two thousand new ways to describe the same product.

Yes, the pictures made it easier. In fact, the pictures were my biggest focus. When, say, faced with some weird breed of dog, I might while away a good hour or so (per breed that is—this gig paid by the hour) surfing the Net seeking out interesting facts about the Norwegian Dach-zhu, the Chinese-Mexican Shar-ua-ua, the Standard French-American Poo-bull, or the Giant Schnaumation.

Then I'd take approximately one of these facts and sprinkle it into an otherwise generic or, better, pulled-from-thin-air description, which I wrote in roughly three minutes.

*The Norwegian Dach-zhu, with his short legs, long body, and wool-like coat, was bred to fetch balls of yarn from underneath the most stubborn pieces of Ikea furniture known to mankind.*

*You'll delight in a collection of twelve amazing Dach-zhus cap-*
*tured in this calendar for your Dach-zhu appreciation!*

Being an absolute dog nut, days I did doggy calendars were actually less unpleasant than All Those Other Days. Like Cat Days.

You know, I was just starting to like cats when I was walloped with an especially large number of cat calendars. Cats being forced to do what cats hate to do. Cats dressed in stupid clothes, wearing ridiculous sunglasses, being coerced into ridiculous cat poses. It was enough (almost) to make me hate cats all over again.

Days when I'd had too much, I'd go on auto-pilot, let my buddy alliteration do the driving:

*This calendar crawling with cute cats can clearly climb into your*
*cat-crazy heart all throughout the year!*

There were other tricks. Certain words were used again and again. This was rather inevitable. For example, when describing mountain calendars, just try not to use the descriptive *craggy*. Or, when dealing with sports teams, I challenge you to come up with a set of sentences that does not include the word *fan*.

But it was always the chicks in bikinis or underwear or pain-fully short cut-offs that got me. I remember one featuring a woman in a skintight jumpsuit, in a garage, allegedly fixing a car. I'm pretty sure she was holding her hammer upside down. (Never mind that, ever since I quit driving cars from the sixties, I find that a hammer is hardly ever necessary anymore for car repair.)

Who was more desperate, I'd sometimes wonder. Me—sitting at my desk, dreaming of writing novels and other great literary stuff, instead describing these barely post-pubescent chicks de-nuded of all body hair? Or them, dreaming of big acting careers while subjecting themselves to said denuding and long hours of making love to the camera while risking nail-breakage due to hammer-holding or thigh-chafing courtesy of ensembles never really designed for the female form to be crammed into in the first place?

Not that it really mattered, mind you. It was just fodder for daydreams, another mini-escape from the drudgery of having to mask the truth, which would've worked just fine for any calendar

I described:

*Look, you need a calendar. This one is as good as any. Just buy it and leave me alone, okay?*

(2002)

## MONEY

I suck with money. I really, really do.

Because whether I am making under thirty thousand dollars (last year, and not the first or last time) or over ninety thousand (1997, a true anomaly, I swear), I always wind up with the same net worth, a number that is forever preceded by a negative sign.

I'm sure if I could afford a financial analyst, she'd have lots of big words for what I'm doing wrong, which, as my friend Alice puts it, is "living like a poor person."

This was precisely Alice's assessment offered recently (free of charge) when I confessed what I did upon receiving an unexpected check in the mail. It was a class-action settlement from MCI, a reward I got for filing paperwork ages ago, mailing it in, and forgetting about it.

When I saw the amount, over thirteen hundred dollars, I knew the right thing to do. Put half in savings and the rest toward debt.

That financially healthy plan was something I thought about a lot as I drove my son around, buying him more treats than he could handle: hair dye and cool clothes and take-out food. To the point he turned to me—this child of mine, so used to living on our typically too small budget—and nervously inquired, "Are you sure this is okay?"

I smiled, big, and nodded.

"THANKS!" he said. His grin and gratitude were totally worth it. I knew I could and would continue to squeak us by as I always do. It's these rare spoiling moments that remind us money can buy at least a little, occasional happiness.

It's happiness I like to share, too, the rare times I am able, suffering as I do, from Pockets Afire, an affliction causing an unstoppable urge to unload my temporary wealth lest I scorch my pants.

So I give away cash and prizes when I can. To friends in need. To the kid's soccer team the year they needed a sponsor. To a bunch of old folks I never met but who I knew needed a printer.

I guess I'm a classic case of the apple falling directly beneath the tree. I grew up poor in a family of eleven living on a truck driver's salary. My mother, infinitely resourceful and deft at stretch, never let us feel the pinch. Hand-me-down clothes started so early that they were a given. Fatty ground beef and ten-cent loaves of day-old bread, a staple. So what? We ate. We were dressed.

Friday nights, my father would come home, paycheck cashed, weighed down with flowers for Mom, vinyl 45s for the kids, fresh fruits and vegetables from the Italian Market in Philly. Less left to pay the debt collectors, to be sure. But then, less for them to take, right?

One year, on my mom's birthday, I asked her for some wisdom. She told me that when she was young, she remembered going into Sears and thinking one day she'd be able to buy any two dresses off the rack, price be damned.

She added that that day had never come, and then she hit me with the story's moral: *When you want something, find a way to get it. Don't wait.*

At least that's how I interpreted it as I sashayed my way into a credit card hole I finally could not get out of. Still, to this day, that take-a-cut-for-me-before-tossing-the-wolves-a-snack attitude prevails.

This is not merely tribute to my parents' ways. The fact that I am both a single mother and an artist—both notorious poverty causes—leave me most often living in a hand-to-mouth situation where my fingertips usually barely brush my lips.

Which is why, invariably, the moment a freelance check does arrive, I go into a trance and wake up in the grocery store checkout line an hour later, so instinctual is it for me to purchase food, quick, lest someone come and take away what's mine.

More often than my family members, the creditors call and write. A couple of years ago a bankruptcy lawyer told me to quit worrying about these calls. It took some practice but I did. I recognize them instantly—they ask for me by my given name, which no one else uses.

Usually I inform them I'm not home. Or I tell them I don't

have a job. Both are lies, but they work in shortening the conversation. I used to give them twenty bucks now and then but they just kept slapping on interest fees to the tune of thousands of dollars per year so I thought I'd rather put that twenty bucks I don't really have somewhere else.

Like shoes for the kid.

Recently, one of my delinquent accounts was passed on to a new owner. This company seems to hire ex-cons and carnies to do their dirty work. One of these ruffians, when informed I had no job, began to ask me about security at my workplace.

I began reiterating not having a workplace but then inquired why he wanted security information. He said, threateningly, they needed to know what they'd be up against when they came to serve me papers. I hung up on him.

Not long after, same company calls. I repeat that I don't have a job. The representative screams that I need to get a job. I hang up on her.

I shrug these people off because I have come to learn what small potatoes I am in their book. They aren't going to serve me papers. They aren't coming for me. Not including the exorbitant rates they keep adding, my true debt to them totals less than ten thousand dollars easily. Their best bet, they think, is to bully me.

I won't be bullied. They don't know it, but I do: I'll get around to them eventually, as I have with other debts.

I do worry about the poorer people, the ones who don't have bankruptcy lawyer friends, the ones who can't steel their way through these wicked phone calls. Because I well remember what it was like before I learned to block them out.

Debt makes people physically ill. Causes deep depressions. Ruins families. Prompts suicides.

In a small magazine I read, *The Sun*, readers responded passionately to an article on debt. One recalled sitting by the phone one day with a gun, planning to blow his brains out into the receiver, let that be the burden of whoever hassled him next.

The phone never rang that day. He came to his senses. He still has that bullet as a reminder.

The U.S. Courts report that the "total bankruptcies filed in calendar year 2001 broke all records, shooting up 19 percent to 1,492,129 in the 12-month period ending December 31, 2001."

Of those, nonbusiness bankruptcies totaled 1,452,030, which was a 19.2 percent increase over 2000. Overall, there has been nearly a 91 percent increase in bankruptcy filings since 1990.

That's a lot of people in trouble. A lot of people who've been made sick by debt. It's a number inflated, in part, because bankruptcy laws are about to change so everyone is in a hurry to file before that happens.

But it's a number that reflects hard times right now, too, in an economy where lots of people are learning anew the definition of tight budget. Where piles of temporarily paper-rich dot-commers got an unwanted financial comeuppance last year, and are coming to understand what it feels like for the rest of us almost all the time, not just in a recession.

One by one, I'm settling these debts of mine. The Visa bill: gone. The IRS debt, well over ten grand: settled and about to disappear. Inspired by these triumphs, I take more baby steps toward eradicating my financial phobias.

I haven't had a credit card in five years, not by choice but default. My credit is ruined. But here is the blessing: I have learned to live entirely without credit. I am learning to live within my means (shopping trips prompted by unexpected windfalls notwithstanding).

My former bank, Worst Bank of America, was forever screwing me with increasing fees and changing rules which were a contributing factor (note: my sucky money skills were the primary factor) in one final, ongoing, insanity-inducing round of bounced checks that left me in an emotional and financial heap on the floor for months.

So I finally made good on my threat to find a better bank, which I did. A credit union. Free checking. No hidden fees. A fresh slate. Am I recording every single transaction in my register and balancing my checkbook weekly? I am.

I even, gasp, hired an accountant. I love the irony of such things—paying someone to assess how much money you don't have. But this was a final component in wiping out a mountain of government debt, and a first step toward better future planning.

For which I'll give myself a little bit of credit—the only credit I hope to have increased interest in from now on.  (2002)

# FOOD

## LUNCH STORY

*What can you say about a career waitress who only meant to take a summer job in high school slinging tomato pies? That she would have committed hari-kari with a rolling pizza slicer had she realized years ago where that job would lead her? That she would discover, too late, this wasn't an adventure, it was a job?*

*What can you say about a life of servitude based on the riotously funny notion that if you bring a properly garnished plate of hostilely prepared food to the customers fast enough, they will find it in their hearts and wallets to leave a little something extra on the table?*

*What can you say about cooks who forget to prepare orders, folks who stiff, and miserable managers? You can say this: Waitressing means always having to say you're sorry.*

I was a waitress for fourteen years, nearly half my life at the time, before I quit for good. I started when I was fifteen years and six months old. I planned on quitting from the time I was fifteen years and seven months old. But from that first order taken, something seized me. Something told me—other aspirations be damned—that if I ever forgot how to balance a tray, I would perish immediately, wind up on the streets.

My eleventh and last gig was in Austin, at the Old Oak Cafe, my final foray into the world of restaurant work, the caboose on a long, long train I rode too far.

Each new job was like stepping on a different car of that train. At first the change seemed refreshing. The seats felt a little different, the view out the window more scenic. Until the realization struck, as it always did: For as different as every restaurant initially felt from the one preceding it, in essence it was precisely the same.

My first day at the Old Oak, I wondered how I had once again ended up in a job I had repeatedly sworn off. Was it genetic? An addiction? A cruel karmic fate inflicted on me for being a fussy patron in a past life? Would my college degree ever be something more than a running joke—"Oh yeah! I got a degree in *English*! Which qualifies me to serve you *English* muffins. Har har." Would I one day find myself at sixty, in a pair of orthopedic shoes, varicose veins bulging through support hose, my arthritic wrist upturned in permanent tray-carrying position, my hair a surreal beehive, working late nights in a truck stop?

There was the compulsory welcome speech. The manager mouthing the words, "We run things differently around here, blah blah blah." My response, as always, was to feign rapt attention, nod agreeably, the whole time wondering: *How much free food can I eat?*

As the Old Oak manager rambled on about the definition of sundry Tex-Mex items, my mind drifted back to Oompah Land, that horrid mall chain of make-believe German cuisine, me twitching and itching in my polyester Frumpy Fraulein ensemble, being instructed on the details of bratwurst and knockwurst, and kraut (canned, thank you), by my Lebanese bosses.

I'd attempt to snap back to reality—"Chili con queso is melted cheese dip with jalapenos"—only to be hurtled back further, this time to Mrs. Crabapple, in that joint in Jersey. During her initial lecture, all I could do was watch the cigarette in her chapped lips bounce up and down with every word, the two-inch-and-growing ash threatening at any second to drop and morph into a tablecloth inferno.

I tried so hard to convince myself that the Old Oak would be different. I would put on that happy face. I would refill that coffee before I was begged to do so. I recalled my grandmother's voice—she who slung hash for thirty years, supporting six kids with her tips. "As long as you wait tables," she told me, "you'll always have cash in your pocket." Not a bad point, and quite a motivating factor considering that, at a good restaurant, you can make more money than at an entry level corporate position.

Not to mention the opportunity to perform. Each new party seated represented a fresh audience. I'd improvise or dig out old favorites in hopes of increasing tips. "Today's my birthday," I'd wink. Or, "Today's my first day," "my last day," or when I was particularly broke or daring, all three.

I called regular coffee leaded and decaf unleaded. I'd look at a licked-clean plate, point to the rind of an orange garnish, and solemnly inquire, "Can I wrap that up for ya?" Often it worked, the twenty percent tips the equivalent of a standing ovation.

Camaraderie was another reason I stuck with it so long. George Burns said, "Happiness is having a large, loving, caring, close-knit family . . . in another city." How true. Still, it has been my experience that one must seek out the dramatic pleasures of dysfunction somewhere. Restaurants are excellent breeding grounds for adopted, soap-operaesque kin. A bizarre vacuum forms around those who must work so closely, day after day. You sleep with your co-workers, drink with them far too late into the evening, kvetch to them and about them.

Nonetheless, after a year or so at the Old Oak, bitterness rivaling that of a four-hour old pot of decaf reared its ugly little head. I began to resent every customer, no matter how nice. I had flashbacks to the Lunch Bucket in Knoxville, where I was fired for finally blowing a gasket one day and informing a return-customer, who had stiffed me, that she sucked. (Her response was that I deserved no tip for failing to bring her a straw to preserve her overabundant lipstick.) I walked out of that job singing "We Shall Overcome," stopping momentarily to pontificate a little more at the horrified customer, my words accompanied by steam enough to heat up meatballs for the entire Swedish Army.

It wasn't just her, either. I realized I could be in Texas one day and New York City the next and still find myself confronting an identical set of idiot customers.

There is The Camper. The Camper lies and says she'll be dining alone, to secure a table during the lunch rush, when it is made very clear that incomplete parties will not be seated. She sits and orders hot herbal tea for hours (and let me tell you what a lengthy process that is, involving saucer, doily, lemon wedge, mini-teapot, cup on the side), secretly waiting to be joined by her new-age counselor/lover/friend/spirit-guide/guru/goofball companion, who will also order herbal tea, once he finally arrives.

They will then sit for three more hours, make out as if they were in a heart-shaped hot tub in the Poconos, and prevent at least four other parties from sitting, eating, tipping and leaving. Finally, they'll drop five dimes on the table (if you're lucky) and flash you a peace sign, which you are prevented, by house policy, from responding to with a hand signal of your own.

The Director takes charge like the supervisor of an overbudgeted Hollywood blockbuster, ordering things only to send them back. One by one. "Take 347! This soup isn't hot enough!" "Take 498! I need another pat of butter!" "Take 973! I said over *EASY!*" Naturally, once the meal is a wrap, the Director wants to make cuts to better fall within his original budget. "You should really remove the charge for that sandwich from my check," he demands, "because it was poorly produced."

There are others, too. Beware the table of five, all men in suits, insisting on separate checks. Behold the eccentric, lonely regulars who like to pretend they are your good buddies, returning not for the food but for the chance to order you around. Grimace at the "friends of the owner," the owner being conveniently absent, unable to verify or decline intimate association. All of these folks think they know what the business is about just because they heard "Alice's Restaurant" on the radio once, ten years ago. They have no idea that we snort about them in the walk-in, nickname them all—Ann Noying, Loser Boy I, Loser Boy II, Brillo-Pad Head.

Waiting on tables all those years warped my mind, leading me to create increasingly bizarre fantasies. One of the best begins, as do many, with me finding myself suddenly and inexplicably wealthy. Do I trot the globe with my new-found fortunes? I do not.

Instead, I round up all of my favorite waitresses of days gone by. There's Jean, the old woman who snarled as she took orders and scared people into tipping her. Paula, who used to plot with me about getting even with the owners of Oompah Land. And all the women I worked with at Riddle's, in the heart of St. Louis.

We don black, Lone Ranger masks and traverse the U.S., seeking the most tired, most deserving waitress we can find in the crappiest restaurant out there. We will be able to tell, just by looking at her, that she needs us badly, though she is so far gone she doesn't realize this herself.

We request her station and order grilled cheese sandwiches. We never complain, even if the bread is soggy, even if it is burnt. When the check comes, we slip a hundred dollar bill (maybe two) under the sugar shaker and disappear into the night.

The wind whistles at our backs, and in the distance we hear a whip-like crack. It is the crack of another egg for another of her grumpy customers. We hear her sigh. We imagine her face as she finds our little gift. And we wish this for her, of her latest customer: *Please, Lord, let him be satisfied.*                                    (1994)

## SEASONAL AFFECTIVE CHEESECAKE

Glancing back across the snow-dappled arc of Yankee Decembers past, I see, as if it were yesterday, the typical Christmas Eve of my youth. My five younger siblings all snug in their beds. Me, finally allowed to stay awake and decorate the tree, sneak the presents out to place beneath it.

Yes, me, finally knowing what really happens on this night, the mystery revealed. Here it is: As *The Bells of St. Mary's* drifts across the screen of the big, wood-encased console, my father, prone and cranky on the couch, snipes irritably at me to *Quit clumping the tinsel, dammit!*

So strong is this memory that I need only envision Ingrid Bergman in a habit and tears spring to my eyes.

It would be a couple of decades before I came to learn Seasonal Affective Disorder is a real affliction with a real name. That my father likely suffers it. That I most certainly do.

But long before this information became clear as the silhouette of eight tiny flying reindeer back-lit by a full moon, somewhere, deep inside, I was aware of it. Boy was I.

I've often felt bad for the way this annual "tradition" worries my friends so. Invariably, two weeks into every December, my phone starts ringing more often than usual: *Are you okay?*

This might get blurted up front, buried in the middle, or wrapped jovially in the closing sentiment: *Well, Merry Christmas! Glad you're okay!* Always though, the question is there.

I am not purposefully grim, miserable, weepy, and (sometimes) fetal with depression on the holidays. Sure it might seem like a good ploy for extra attention. But really that's the last thing you want when you're depressed. So check the list twice and cross Crying-for-Attention off the naughty side.

While not intentionally naughty, I realize my holiday disdain is by no stretch *nice,* either. I dislike that I make my friends uncomfortable. I wish not to create memories that will provoke my son, Mr. Even Keel and Holiday Happy, to publicly lambaste, years hence, the misery he suffered listening to his mother bitching about the ill-placement of raisin belly buttons on the ginger folk.

Thus, over the years, at first sarcastically but now, oddly, in a sort of sincere way, I have developed and honed my personal method of surviving what I am inclined to call the Hellidays.

The main component of my "cure" began some twenty-five years ago with a simple, custardy cheesecake recipe procured by one of my elder sisters from the Home Economics files at Gateway Regional High School. No doubt this recipe came from one of those magazines with headlines that blare: *Lose Ten Pounds While Devouring This Cheesecake* and/or *Bake Him This Cheesecake and He'll March You to the Altar!*

My feminist issue with the roots of the recipe aside, I must say: it makes a damn fine dessert. In the past quarter century, my seven sisters and I have surely have made over a thousand of these.

My own cheesecake baking probably seized me as full-on annual tradition the December my son was born. It was 1990, and my actions were greatly influenced by the fluctuating hormones that accompany new motherhood and the fact that I was iced into my St. Louis home with a newborn.

Some afternoons, I'd wake from a nap to notice a half-dozen or more cheesecakes on the counters. *Now where had these come from?*

This tradition grew until, eventually, some Christmases would arrive to see me having popped perhaps thirty of the things out in a week. My motto: "Keep the oven full and there's no room for your head!"

My friends didn't really care that I hadn't earmarked any particular cake for any particular person. The deal became: stop by during the Beat Back the Blues Baking Bonanza and net yourself a cheesecake. Now those annual calls to check on my mental health come with an additional question: *Hey, you aren't making cheesecakes this year by any chance, are you?*

Everyone wants one. For two years running I even sent some to the home of the ex-boyfriend's mother I never met. (Yes, even post-breakup I try to impress their mothers. Why? *WHY?*)

Then there was the one delivered to my therapist, as I shared the tale of my kitchen mania. She told me the baking was nice and all, but really, if I was making that many cheesecakes, I might want to examine my Obsessive Compulsive tendencies and accept that it was okay to cut back.

That was what she said *before* she ate hers. A week or so later, I got a letter from her: *I know I said you don't need to make so many cheesecakes but . . . well . . . if you do make them next year, please keep me in mind.*

Quite by accident then, the cheesecakes have come to make me feel useful at Christmas. Useful is, I think, about the best feeling one can achieve in life. And so now, as the hellidays again approach, though depression will ring the doorbell, and though I will show it in, I will also force it to sit at the kitchen table and watch me go, go, go. Depression—hardly a fan of productivity and happy cinnamonny smells and cheerful, dessert-seeking drop-in company—will, I'm sure, shrink away disappointed then at its inability to knock me on my batonkis.

Perhaps inspired by friends' enthusiastic cheesecake response, I guess one year I just got to thinking, *What the hell, why stop with cheesecake?*

So out comes the gingerbread recipe. The loose-leaf is old, covered with comforting food stains dating back to God-only-knows-when. I make gingerbread people and stars and candy canes. I buy tubes of icing and six-packs of beer and encourage cheesecake seekers to pull up a chair, stay awhile, decorate these cookies and hang them on the stupid tree already, will you?

Laughter fills the room. People stay. More people arrive. Maybe the Scrabble board gets pulled out. Maybe, unable to stop myself, I make a pot of that spicy red lentil soup everyone loves. Maybe, if I am on Vicodin (as I was one year, courtesy of dental work), I get really crazy and assemble all the necessary ingredients for a make-your-own-holiday-cards session.

Somehow, then, my sloppy little on-a-tilt rental cottage has become some unintended home to holiday happiness. This was never my intent. If anything, these orphan gatherings evolved only to insure my other holiday-loathing friends would have sanctuary, freedom to voice ill feelings of unwelcome festivities.

Don't worry. I won't slap on here some you-can-be-happy-on-the-holidays-if-you-just-open-your-heart ending. I still wish those of us who wanted to escape the fuss could. But I have learned that The Season is much like some peppy ex-lover you futilely try to avoid, only to have him appear everywhere you turn—happy, rested, well dressed, and oblivious to your pain.

As I deal with such exes, so cope I with December. That is, I do what I can: keep busy, wince my way through, call my friends. These friends laugh at my curmudgeonly complaints and point out—sometimes speaking with mouths full of cheesecake—that I've become some perverse holiday queen. Which makes me laugh a laugh I hadn't intended.

But who cares, right? At least I'm laughing. Mistake it, if you must, for holiday cheer. Whatever gets you through, that's what I say.

### CHEESECAKE RECIPE

*Crust*:

> 1/4 pound of butter
> 6 tablespoons sugar
> 1 teaspoon baking powder
> 2 cups flour
> 2 eggs

*Crust Directions:*

1. Clear a good spot on the kitchen table or counter for a bowl. (Pushing delinquent bills aside and dropping cats onto the floor if necessary. Don't worry, the cats always land on their feet and you will, too, once you get caught up on those bills.)

2. Even though my ex-boyfriend Andy's wife Kelly tells me it is a culinary sin to do so, I say go ahead and nuke the butter in your microwave 'til it's good and melted. Then pour it in the bowl.

3. Add the sugar, and cream sugar and butter until it's the way it should be or the phone rings.

4. Throw in the eggs and baking powder (hint: best to remove shells from eggs). Now mix until smooth (my mom's notes say SLOWLY but I don't always listen to my mom).

5. Add flour. At this point, you might want to ditch the electric mixer, because the crust dough gets pretty stiff. Don't be shy—use your hands, that's what they're there for. Mix it up real good. Then cut the dough ball in half.

6. Put one half (left or right, your choice) into the center of an 8" *cake* pan. (For years we used square, disposable aluminum pans until we decided the round ones were *Much Klassier*.) Now flatten that ball and slowly smush it toward the sides and then up the sides. It's okay if there are a ton of fingerprints, and it's also okay if the dough is pretty thin because it will rise some in the oven. This is tricky the first time or two, but once you finish your first batch of thirty, you'll be an old pro. Don't get discouraged. If you want, use a small, smooth juice glass as a mini-rolling pin to help.

*Filling:*
2 eight-ounce packages of cream cheese
1 1/2 cups of sugar
4 eggs
3 tablespoons cornstarch
1 1/4 teaspoons lemon juice
1 teaspoon vanilla
3 cups of milk (2 percent is fine if you want)
Cinnamon

*Directions:*
Make sure you use a real big bowl for this, or, if you don't have a real big bowl, use a big pot. Cream the cream cheese and sugar together. If you ever got your finger stuck in beaters before and know how painful that can be, take a moment while you're mixing to be glad you don't make *that* mistake anymore.

Add the eggs. (Again, it's best to remove the shells first.)

Add the cornstarch (weird, I know), the lemon juice (I use fresh lemon juice), and the vanilla. Now beat it some more 'til it's smooth.

Add the milk. As you do, you'll realize why it was so important to use a big pot. Pretty messy, right? I told you. Now just beat it, beat it, beat it, beat it. And see if you can do that without getting Michael Jackson stuck in your head. This is one step where I do listen to my mom who says, "Electric Mixer Will Make It Lighter" in her handwriting (which looks a lot like mine. How does that happen?). You want this part fluffy.

Pour into pans*, sprinkle with cinnamon, and bake for around an hour at 350 degrees. I say "around" an hour because you know your oven better than I do. You'll know when it's done—it sort of gels and you might even see a few tiny cracks across the top which is perfectly fine—you're not Martha Stewart, okay?

Let the cheesecake cool. Keep in fridge.

Repeat this entire process fifteen times to get yourself through the hellidays.

*HELPFUL TIPS: You can make your life easier by pouring the filling into a pitcher first. Now take the pans (with the crusts but not with the filling) and set them on the rack in your oven. Okay NOW pour the filling in and very carefully slide the rack into place. This saves major spillage. (2001)

# SOBERING THOUGHTS

## ST. LOUIS

I am thinking of a metaphor, trying to capture what St. Louis was for me. My mind keeps coming back to this: *house.*

It is a dream metaphor, a cliché, nothing at all original to it. To dream of house is to dream of self.

In my real life, the most vivid dream I ever had was in a hotel in Memphis. I was there on assignment to interview a psychic.

The night before the interview, lulled by tall draughts in a Hyatt bar filled with the ironic singing of countless birds in countless cages scattered throughout, I retired to my room, drew the heavy curtains—the sort that can make noontime nighttime—and fell asleep.

As I slept, a house filled my head. It was a big house and in disarray. I was packing. There was luggage.

And then came the rats. They swarmed this nightmare house, outfitted in helmets made of those shiny ashtrays—you know the sort. They look like red or yellow or green foil. Festive ashtrays for Christmas cigarettes if there were such a brand. Perfect little rat helmets.

Alarmed, I awoke, but not really. After fumbling like a rat myself through the maze of a pitch-black, unfamiliar hotel room, no idea where I was, I flipped on the bathroom light and nearly dropped over dead when I spotted her. It took a minute until I really woke up and then another until I recognized her.

Me. In the mirror.

The next day I told the psychic my dream. She's the one who told me that house is symbol for self. She told me about the rats, too. Rats in dreams, she said, indicate stubborn habits. The rats you saw, they wore helmets. Extra stubborn.

That was thirteen years ago. Six months after I met that woman, I left Tennessee. Packed the station wagon, left behind lease and furniture (broken, both). Moved to St. Louis, thinking four things along the drive: new love, new life, hot shower, cold beer.

Five hundred miles later, I am in the shower washing off the smell of hangover and sour whipped cream from the going away shots and pie in the face provided by my coworkers. And as I apply suds to my body, so I imbibe suds into my system, a cold Budweiser on bathtub's edge beside the soap.

If you are an alcoholic or have ever known one up close, you can guess where this story goes. I could quibble with you about whether my eventual, exponential increase in alcohol intake, and my ultimate decision to quit—moderation being impossible for me—classifies me as alcoholic or problem drinker.

It doesn't matter.

What matters in my life, what matters regarding the drinking, are three things.

First: I had more, far more, than I ever should have, for far longer than I should have, but I stopped.

Second: my aforementioned love (now former, because of this very thing), for whatever reasons, has had and continues to have far more than he should have.

Third: only time will tell where along the drinking fence our son will choose to sit (or fall) once he reaches the age his father began drinking (thirteen) or maybe the age I began (fifteen) (or whenever it happens that temptation calls out to him at a party, in a bar, in a basement after school, in a dorm, at a wedding, in a restaurant).

It's everywhere. It's especially everywhere in St. Louis. That's what I think. Or maybe that's just who I was then, what I was doing. *Drinker at height of drinking.*

The house I think of as metaphor for this town is a house that looks quite normal, quite nice. Some sunshine and reading nooks. A good amount of space. And a locked closet down the basement. A locked closet with a tiny little lock—I could pick it with Barbie's toothpick, if Barbie came with toothpicks.

It is Pandora's bar and it comes standard with the house I remember as St. Louis.

God I loved to drink. McClain's, CBGB's, Webster Bar and Grill, the counter at Imo's, after hours at Riddle's (where I waited tables in the Loop). At the parties, in the yards, on the steps—everywhere we went we drank. That's all there was too it. Get up. Do something. Do something else. Start drinking.

I don't know if everyone in St. Louis really drinks like this. This is just the memory I have. It's like meeting one crazy Frenchman in your lifetime, at a grocery store in Indiana. And he scratches his balls constantly and talks only of green bananas. You know better, don't you, than to think that all Frenchmen must scratch their balls ceaselessly and blather on foolishly of unripe fruit? But you can't help it—somewhere the image sticks. Somehow, the message gets through: all the French must be this way.

I think of St. Louis, the house, the cliché. In my memory, everyone is drunk always, or else making preparation to get that way. I come back to visit sometimes, bring my child to see his father, whose hands tremble always now, though he is only thirty-five.

There are still the parties. One thing is missing now. This man, the one I used to go with. He stays at home and drinks. It's not a social thing anymore. It's something like that Neil Young line about the same thing that can make you live can kill you in the end. It's killing him. It's keeping him alive. He stops, his body seizes and convulses and might just quit. He keeps going: It will quit.

We give up hope. We do not give up hope.

Now and then we point the car north, we go to visit, we hope. Maybe he'll be better. Maybe . . .

When I get to St. Louis, it burns me every time, like a shot of tequila on an empty, early-morning stomach. I am fascinated by this city. And I am mortified. I drive up Big Bend toward the Loop and I know I have driven this road drunk, blind drunk. Not once. Not by mistake. Purposefully. As a matter of course. Go to work. Get drunk. Get more drunk. Drive home. Night after night, week after week.

Every street I drive down, every friend I visit, I remember. The time we got drunk. The other time we got drunk. The time we got less drunk, but still . . . and we put the kid in the back seat—*Hey, he was in his car seat!*—and away we drove.

I go to a party this past December and there they all are, everyone but him—he who is home alone, getting drunk. I feel odd now, among these friends and family I used to match and surpass at drinking. I stand, sober, not knowing what to do with my hands. It will be another month before I quit smoking, and so at least I have that for now.

We greet each other and I note that most of us have an extra layer of bloat now—is this just age, or is this the beer? And everyone, they'll head straight to the fridge, cram in their offering: no one shows up with less than twelve Busch cans or bottles of something.

A funny, sick, twisted feeling grabs me then. I swallow it, hold it down, the way you hold down the vomit that threatens to escape esophagus, blanket the bar, unless you shut your lips and gulp backwards as you stumble for the bathroom, pray to get your head in the toilet in time.

The feeling: I will want to beg someone to please, please, take me to a pub. A shitty place. Like Sweet Pea's, where I used to love to go. Where a friend once pointed to a drunken woman—I swear she was nine months pregnant and doing shots—fighting with her man at the pool table, skulls about to get cracked. "Look," said my friend, "Hoosier foreplay."

(Another night, this same friend will take me out, once I'm drunk, and put me—in my mini-skirt, no underwear—atop his motorcycle. He will drive me to the middle of the city, get off, and tell the drunken me there's only one way we're getting back, and that's if I'm driving. And so I do—I learn, right there, liver fried, crotch exposed, to shift those gears and slide us back to the bar. Another round, please, to celebrate my first drive on a motorcycle!)

And at the pub I want to beg to go to, here is what I want to do. I want to remember what it feels like to get blind drunk in St. Louis. I want to sit there and order pitcher after pitcher and drink until I puke. I want to get even with the universe for taking my love from me. I want to toast the gods for letting me escape. I want to be able to drink until I fall over and then I want to get up and feel nothing the next day.

I have another soda.

When I first moved to St. Louis, I had no plan. No job lined up. No money more than the hundred I'd brought. He lived with his parents and they weren't exactly thrilled at the prospect of us setting up house under their roof. We had love and beer then. That seemed logical and more than enough.

Some friends and a sibling had a rental house they were going to move in to just as soon as they fixed it up. It was a house with potential. Needed some paint. A little love.

We could stay there awhile, they said. We did. Empty house

save for one mattress. A place to sit and drink. A place to sleep drunk.

It took a while for the pattern to emerge. Mornings, hungover, sometimes I could find only one red Ked. Now that was funny—had I been *that* drunk? I could've sworn I'd taken my shoes off together, set them side by side.

Then we noticed. Teeth marks, on the shoes.

We weren't alone in that house. There was a rat. Strong and stubborn. Relentless.

Capable of splitting up a pair. (2001)

## VISITING JAMES

The last time my son saw his father, we were all in St. Louis. That's where Henry was born, where we lived until he was nine months old, where James returned after our relationship ended eight years ago.

The last time we saw James was last summer. St. Louis was the first official stop on a several-thousand-mile road trip, in our a/c-free Toyota. We got there in the middle of the night, stayed with James. That's usually how it goes. We stay with him when we visit, he stays with us when he visits.

Here's how else it usually goes, and did, in fact, go last summer. Not long into our stay, this time less than twelve hours, James had a grand mal seizure.

This time, I saw it. I don't know why, but all the other ones over the years, I've managed to miss. For example, I'll leave the two of them—always with another adult, just in case—for a quick errand and James will go into convulsions.

Each time, while Henry has been close, the other adult has managed to whisk him to another room, where he'll hear the thrashing, maybe hear James' head hit a wall, a counter, the floor, but never actually see it.

Seizures are not something you want to witness. I knew this without having to find out the hard way. I found out the hard way anyway.

A scene from last summer: Henry and James are upstairs in

James' sister's house. I am in the basement. I hear a shout, "Get up here!" and I race up the basement stairs, fling open the door. Try to fling it open. I can't. A body, on the floor, is blocking it.

Through the crack, I see James, prone, his brother-in-law straddling him. Confused—are they pretending to wrestle for Henry? But no, that was an urgent voice beckoning me . . . a voice now informing, "You can't get up this way!"

I turn, race for the basement door, up the outdoor stairs, in through the kitchen. It's over by then. James is lying there, taut, muscles still strung tight from the episode which, like the others, he will have no recollection of. I kneel down beside him. His eyes are wild. He has no idea where he is, who I am, who he is. I hold his hand and say, over and over and over, "It's okay. It's okay."

"I'm scared!" he screams. "Who are you? Are you going to kill me?" I feign calm. *Itsokayitsokayitsokay. I love you.* And then I make the choice. My son? His father?

Brother-in-law and I lug James to the car. Which hospital this time? We're running out of options. James has no money, no insurance, and, it sometimes seems, no hope. Because it is perceived that this condition of his is self-induced, because he comes from pull-yourself-up-by-the-bootstraps stock, no one likes to think of the addiction as a disease.

*It's a weakness. He could quit anytime he wanted. He doesn't want to.*

It's a Saturday night in the hospital, the Cardinals are playing, the ER is packed. I stand in front of James. He's sitting in a wheelchair, puking bile, because there is no food in his stomach, probably hasn't been for days. I hold the plastic dish, catch the mucus. *Itsokayitsokayitsokay.*

Call Henry. "He's going to be fine, honey. Fine. I love you. I'll call back soon."

Standing, waiting, worrying, I am not without guilt. That afternoon, while James played with Henry, I sat out back sharing beers with the others. It's a terrible game I play around James. A game I used to play.

James has seizures because he has severe alcoholism. When he quits drinking, usually before Henry comes to visit, his body cannot handle the thing it is missing, the thing it has come to rely on. When I see James, I always want to drink. Out of view. But as some proof. Of what? Of my nervousness? Of the fact it got him and did not get me?

Or maybe it's like this: Maybe it's like, "Okay, James, you send no money. You take no responsibility. I raise our child and have for all these years. Okay, it's your turn. You play. I'll drink." Maybe, just maybe, there was some spite in those beers. Is that sick?

Alcohol will do that to you.

They take him back, put him on a bed. I'm in the waiting room. A preacher greets a family at the automatic doors. This can't be good.

After a while, I am allowed to see James. He's dazed. He doesn't look good. The doctor says he's fine, no DTs, he just needs to be hydrated. I am doubtful. The doctor exits. I'm standing there, looking at the man I sometimes think was my one true love. And it happens. Again.

A seizure is not something you want to see. He is blue, arching, veins bulging. I run for help. I run back to be with him. They chase me out.

Henry and I have scheduled stops down the road, across the country. Henry does not want to leave St. Louis, not until his father is let out of the hospital. I take him to see James the second day? The third?

In the foyer of this hospital is a statue of St. Louis. St. Louis looks an awful lot like modern-day renderings of Christ. St. Louis has a beggar kneeling at his feet. He is handing the beggar a loaf of bread, a brownish round thing. "Look," says Henry, "Jesus is giving that man a kidney." This is Henry, interpreting how he thinks things go in hospitals.

James is obstinate, yells at me for not giving him a cigarette. In short, James is an ass. The doctor and nurses each in turn refer to him as my husband. I explain: No, he's not. I explain he's Henry's dad. We're just visiting. Some seem confused. Why are we here? Why would we care? Is it even right for me to show my son his father in this condition?

I have no idea. And this is not my version of *Scared Straight*, trying to keep my son from his father's fate (though it is a fear I entertain often).

This is the man I once loved so hard, the man who, looking back over a sea of men, was always the most gentle. The man who loved me. For myself. For my brain. Who didn't care when I gained weight. Who didn't care when I lost it. We loved each other. You should've seen us.

Should've seen us in the bars. After shifts, at the counter of the restaurant we worked in together. Throwing back those beers. Staying late. Laughing with everyone. You should've seen us. We could drink a rugby team under the table.

James never stopped. I tried. Lasted a few months. Tried. Lasted a little longer. It went on like this. Me feeling all that guilt. Me wanting my drink. Me knowing I could've just as easily been the one taken.

The day they discharge him from the hospital, we are there. He's told the doctor he isn't doing rehab again. I excuse the doctor. A nurse takes Henry off down the hall, heaps upon him her older boys' clothes, cool stuff, a satin soccer jacket, things she'd brought to pass down to the other nurses' boys.

I face off with James. *You are being an idiot*, I say. Long ago I tried to back off. Stop yelling. Stop guilting. Just stop. This is his mountain. I tried to climb it for him through our relationship. Tried to carry him on my back. Me as martyr. Me as failure.

In the end, he agrees to go. The only place left—given his track record, his poverty, his ruined credit—is a bed I find in a place in the bowels of the bowels of that city. Henry and I stand, in a street full of broken glass and broken men, and we step through the gate, into the smell that is a halfway house for destitute drunks who do not get the luxury of air-conditioning, even in the worst heat wave of the century.

"It's time to tell Daddy goodbye," I say, and step aside.

I quit drinking the third day of this new century. It wasn't hard this time. I don't miss it.

Never say never, this I know. But the thrill isn't there anymore. The medicine I took for twenty years to mask the pain of depressions that seized me, as real as the convulsions that seize my boy's father, no longer works. Not even short-term. I can't bear it anymore. What it has done to me, to us. Wince back at what was lost. I am the lucky one. I am not smug or cavalier about stepping away like that. James would step away, too. I really think so. But he can't.

It got him. It could've been me.

Henry and I do physical stuff now. This is how I fight back my demons. He skates. I walk. We take martial arts together. Recently, after the last bout of depression, I looked for something new. A couple of months ago, we started yoga.

Our first night, after the stretching, the feeling of parts I do not know I have, we are granted reprieve. *Lie still. Close your eyes. Visualize.* I balk, slightly, the cynic in me not wanting to do this goofy exercise. But I close my eyes. I listen.

*Go to a stream,* the teacher tells us. *You're with an old friend. Someone you really care about.* She describes a scenario so vivid, to my own surprise I am there, faraway. With an old lover, a good friend now. It's taken years. We have so much fun. Tears spring to my eyes.

Leaving class a little while later, Henry asks, "Who were you talking to?"

Confused, I look around me. "No one, what do you mean?"

"In the thing," he says, and I realize now he means the exercise.

"An old friend," I say. "How about you?"

"My dad," he answers, and describes the fun they had. It wasn't an exercise. He was there. James, too.

Now, sometimes at night, I send Henry away. *Lie down,* I say, *close your eyes.* I give him wings. I send him to snowy mountains which, miraculously, are centered with warm green fields. Sometimes he asks me to slow down, because he's really going where I send him. He needs a minute to get there.

And when he comes back, I ask him how it was, was it fun?

"Oh yeah," he says. "I was with my dad."                    (2000)


## ZEN AND THE ART OF NOT DRINKING

Buddha, Santa Claus, and Elvis simultaneously appeared in my life recently. I was not partaking in any mind-altering substances. This really happened, one of those fleeting moments when, if you're incredibly lucky, you happen to be in the right place at the right time, eyes open, ready to receive.

Buddha got the ball rolling on May 26. That was Vesak Day, a celebration of the birth, enlightenment, and death of Buddha. I spent this day meditating and comingling with Buddhists, Buddhist monks, and other curious folks like myself at a beautiful monastery in Augusta, Missouri, near St. Louis.

I found out about the celebration in the *St. Louis Post-Dispatch*. I happened to be reading that paper because Henry and I are on our annual road trip right now, which always entails a stop in St. Louis to visit Henry's paternal relatives, chief among them his dad, James, who moved back here after our breakup in '93.

These visits have not always been easy. In fact, most often, they've been incredibly hard. Like me, James started hitting the bottle as a young teen. For some reason, it got him worse than it got me. While I was able to quit after twenty years and a number of attempts, James kept at it even after he began succumbing to alcohol-related grand mal seizures.

As the years passed, and attempts at rehab failed, increasingly it seemed like each visit would be our last, that the next drive north would be for James's funeral.

I never lied to Henry about his father's addiction. And when, as a very little kid, he once asked if James was going to die from drinking, I told him, as gently as I could, that this was something we had to try to prepare for.

Some might counsel to keep a child away from a parent this sick or at least disguise the gravity of the situation. I never could. I have a relationship with The Truth that borders on obsessive.

Which is why I also never gave the kid Santa Claus, the Easter Bunny, or any of those other creatures. At least not in the traditional sense. I just couldn't bring myself to tell him they existed. I did explain the spirit of Christmas. And one or two years, when he asked if we could go ahead and have Santa—just pretend— I complied.

We did hit a rough patch once when Henry lost a tooth and wanted a dollar. I told him we'd already gone over the nonexistence of the Tooth Fairy. He got visibly upset. I felt guilty, like why can't I be a normal parent for once and just give the kid a moment of magic. In the end, he got a buck and tiny note under the pillow, written in microscopic font:

Dear Henry, Sometimes it pays to believe. The Tooth Fairy

I forgot all about that for years until an event the other day reminded me that sometimes it really does pay to believe.

We'd just left St. Louis, having said good-bye to James. As do all farewells, this one left a sadness. But one of a different sort. Because a year ago—who can say how or why—James finally found a rehab program that works for him. He is sober now, fully awake and aware for the first time in nearly twenty-five years. He calls Henry all the time. Child support comes like clockwork, extra when times are tight. Times we visit, I can leave the two of them alone together for long stretches, something entirely new for me.

There is still much to learn and understand—individually and together. But we are getting better at it. I recognize that I am forever trying to impose my patented False Sense of Control™ on James— micromanaging every minute he and Henry spend together. He understands this comes from years of me having to be totally in charge. I practice letting loose the reins a little more each time. He works on showing me this is now a perfectly safe thing to do.

It's a miracle, yes, and not a small one. So now our reluctance to leave James is about wanting to stay, not fearing it's the last time we'll see him alive.

Still, we had to go. Because Henry and I had been invited (as the press—Hen being my assistant) to the wedding of a couple marrying on The Legend, a famous roller coaster at HolidayWorld, this amazing family-owned theme park tucked down a country road in Indiana.

In Santa Claus, Indiana, to be precise.

Before the wedding, milling around with the rest of the press, who should approach us but Santa Claus himself, who handed me his card, explained the free-soft-drinks-all-the-time policy at the park, and discussed his sensitivity to the sun. (He was a red-head, you know, before he turned all snowy up top.)

The wedding party's car chugged up to the top of a mighty coaster hill, where it ground to a halt. There, after heralding them with a love song, an Elvis impersonator officiated, announcing over the PA the great reverent occasion that marriage is. Vows exchanged, the couple flew down the hill then proceeded to Zoombabwe, the biggest enclosed waterslide in the country, where they "took the plunge" in their formal wear. (Elvis declined joining in, noting his white jumpsuit was not a rental.)

At some point I snapped a picture of Henry with Elvis and Santa together, a look of joyous disbelief (the good kind) in the child's eyes.

At three P.M., bending my own always-the-complete-truth rule, I lured him to park's entrance under false pretense of needing to see the publicist. Approaching the gates, he did a double take.

"There's my dad," he said, rightfully confused as we were two hundred miles east of Missouri.

"I know," I said and hugged him.

It was our big plan, James and me. Together, as parents who have learned (and are still learning) a whole lot of parenting (and life) the hard way, we conspired to surprise our son, who has over-looked our errors and loved us both full-heartedly from the get-go. He had no clue, telling James good-bye, that they'd meet again the next day, for a chance to ride rides, hang out, act silly.

Be normal.

This was not making up for the past or planning for the future. It was a chance, as Buddha would say, to "just be." Our first time, in eleven years, the three of us together on the neutral territory of Santa Claus, Indiana, momentarily free from some of the harsher realities we've known.

At day's end, waiting for the hilarious high-dive act to begin, I fished from my bag *A Little Book of Zen,* which I'd brought along. During our week in St. Louis, my budding curiosity in Buddhism had been the funny source of gentle teasing from James, with him leaving me little notes filled with faux-Zen "wisdom."

Now I thumbed through the pages, found a real saying by Sri Aurobindo that suited our lives. "By your stumbling, the world is perfected."

We concurred that, if this were true, certainly the two of us had contributed greatly to the planet's perfection.  (2002)

## MOM

Whoever said you can't go home again was wrong. Sure you can. I've done it bunches since I left eighteen years ago.

Eighteen years. My magical measurement. Eighteen years with

my parents. Eighteen years on my own. A few weeks ago, I turned thirty-seven. Next set of eighteen years.

I went home. Time to try again.

Here is how it looked, often enough, other visits back: I arrive. I am stressed. My father and I find some new twist on our lifelong mutual grudge. We go at it.

Here's how else it looked: I storm out, a vision of my mother's sad face my only souvenir.

Other times I stay put. I hide behind a book, a laptop, a bottle of booze. Or I hop the train to New York City, book-ending these escapes with fleeting hellos and good-byes. Or I present my son as goodwill ambassador. Watch from the shadows.

Only once do I really stick around. Two months. I return having lived up to my father's prediction that the one destination I'd never struggle finding was trouble. I am twenty-two. Fresh out of college. Recently split from boyfriend. Pregnant.

I had only wanted to get away to something, anything else. Back, I fell into line. Resumed the old mall job. Lived under their roof again, in a spare apartment they offered. Contemplated single motherhood. Inquired at the state college about that teaching certification idea I'd shunned when my high school counselor claimed it my fate.

And then, one November night, my mother is pressing heating pad against my back, as I writhe in the anguish of miscarriage.

I stay a few more weeks. Take up knitting. Sit in my bedroom weeping, knotting a tight, angry scarf. Tension mounts. Volcano blows. Me and daddy. At it again. Away I storm. Mental snapshot: my mother, so sad.

The story repeats through the years, albeit less dramatically. Sometimes, I stay away for years. I cannot reconcile myself to this. I cannot stand his criticisms. Can't bear her worried face.

I let them down some more. I document my anger and my pain, put these things in public places. As my mother censored what I read in my childhood, I attempt to return the deed. She sees my words anyway. Some of them. Not all of them. Enough.

Whoever said to write you must pretend they're all dead was right. But they forgot to mention the part about how, if they aren't, and they read it, a little part of them just might die.

I keep writing. Privately one year I write letters. Two. Mother.

Father. To him I say little more than *How dare you?* To her I say so much more. Was she complicit? Why did I never hear her defend me? Did she agree with him?

Or was she a product of her generation—where men rule and women shut up? I want to know these things. I want to know why she loved him more.

She writes back. It's not more or less, she tells me. It's different sorts of love. She reminds me how hard he worked, all those hours, outside, breaking his back to support nine kids. Fair exchange, she defends, against my accusation that she always catered to him. She is angry with me. I've done it again.

We never reach a truce. Sometimes, the silence is months long. Always it is deafening.

I go home this last time determined. I am a grown-up now. I miss my mother. I want her to understand. For years his words of fault-finding drowned out her encouragement. His "You'll fail," taking precedence over her "You can do whatever you want."

I am starting to understand that, actually, I *can* do whatever I want. I'm still not entirely sure how. I'm working on it.

I want to speak my mind. I want to not make my mother sad. These goals seem mutually exclusive. I think about what I believe were her wishes for me: calmer path, real job, good man. I think about my wishes for her: go to college, cut loose, let him cook his own damn supper.

I walk into my parents' house. My mother hugs me hard. My father stays away. This is our unspoken peace agreement: wide berth, common silence. I choose, for once, to interpret his avoidance as non-hostile. He is giving me my turn with her.

I take it.

In her sitting room, grandbaby number twenty-three, two months old, sprawls across her lap, gnaws happily on a knuckle. I recognize this room. I look down at the knitting I have recently taken up again. This is full circle. My mother's sitting room, my former bedroom, that place we spent a sleepless November night, fifteen years ago.

She shows me her new computer. I promise not to do anything weird to it as I reach for the mouse. I promptly do something weird to it. Move away, control the damage, resume knitting.

As with other families, nothing is uncomplicated in ours. I

choose my words carefully, try to stick to things safe. She mentions she can read me regularly now with her computer. I cringe. Beat around bush. Finally ask if she has seen that one essay, the one I hope she hasn't.

She says she loves me anyway, meaning yes. I say I want to cry. She says don't.

I never convinced her, she never convinced me. Not of the hopes we had for each other. But we have convinced ourselves, each other, of something else. That we are happy with our respective choices. We are stubborn on this point. We have spent years proving ourselves to one another. Finally, I think we agree.

Whoever said time heals all wounds was only halfway right. But time has smeared a little Vaseline over hindsight's lens. I won't forget the storms past, but I know the relief of what it feels like to have survived.

Her voice comes to me now much louder than it used to. It drowns out the doubts he had—his fears disguised as disdain. Pity for her stretching the budget and five pounds of ground beef over a week is replaced with awe. Memories of her sewing—did she ever sleep?—amaze me. We could not afford to buy new clothes. And so she bought cheap ends of fabric bolts, insistent, nonetheless, that something new would be worn first day of school, Easter, First Communion.

*You seem so calm,* she says. *I am,* I tell her. I have brought nothing extra on this trip—no work, no books, no booze, no train tickets. I am here to sit. Still. To catch up a little with my mother.

I wonder if she hopes for some movie-of-the-week ending. My father and I at peace at last. Discussing our mutual love of music. Laughing over something. Anything.

Whoever said that good things come to those who wait was also only halfway right. You have to consider definition of terms. Good things don't always equal happy endings.

Good things might just mean cease-fire. (2001)

# HISTORY

# MARY, MARY, SO CONTRARY

A short story: So, like, once upon a time, there's this young woman. She feels rejected by her family. She doesn't date much. In her early twenties, she holds a number of jobs deemed *appropriate* for women: like caregiver for an old lady and nanny for some kids. She's not too happy. She writes down her ideas. She likes especially to assert the rights of women. She thinks marriage is silly. She starts to get published. Some people think she's radical. She suffers depression. She gives birth without the "benefit" of marriage, which causes a bit of scandal. Later, rather abruptly, she marries another man.

Wait, is this me, once again, rehashing my life? Actually no. The woman I speak of was born over two hundred years ago.

Meet Mary Wollstonecraft, the woman often credited with the birth of feminism. A chick so wacky she actually thought it was a good idea to educate girls. A gal so liberal she dared suggest that men wrongly strained to keep women in the trivialized role of, well, homemakers, mere objects for their sexual desires and vessels for carrying their children.

I studied Wollstonecraft as part of earning a (go ahead and laugh at the irony) *minor* in Women's Studies. Impressed with her work, I incorporated her into a paper I wrote for Dr. Smith in the lit department (my major). I'd been assigned some readings on Dorothy Wordsworth in Smith's class and thought it would be fun to compare the two women.

Dorothy took a very different route from Mary, who was her contemporary. Separated as a child from her siblings, as an adult Dot seized a chance to reunite with her brother William. (Remember him?) As I understand it, Dorothy was majorly psyched to put herself at Bill's beck and call. He wandered the hills and dales by day, composing lovely poems in his head that would gain him much acclaim. Dot stayed at home, tending the garden, mending Bill's clothes, ironing them to perfection, and, once her adored bro dragged himself home, taking dictation for him.

Seems Dorothy had a pretty good way with words herself, words she somehow managed to find time to write in between all her chores. But she was a little low in the self-esteem department. She did not want to be published. In fact, probably would have preferred to be called Dorothy Words-worthless. Bill, however, riffling through his sister's notebooks, *knew* she had too much talent to waste. So, thoughtful guy that he was, he took her words and showed them to the world. In his works.

So I wrote a sort of silly paper in which I wondered what would have happened if Mary had spirited Dot off to a mead hall one night—you know, a sort of precursor to Thelma and Louise—bought her a couple of drinks, and convinced her she was a fool for being Bill's doormat. I went on to rewrite Dorothy's journals, as if this event had occurred, and the entries went something like this:

[15th May, Thursday: A coldish dull morning—hoed the first row of peas, weeded, etc. etc. Sat hard mending until evening. I try hard to be patient with the mending, but since reading dear Mary's work I can barely sit still. I wish Wm. would mend his own clothes. I have come up with a plan to teach him. Tonight I sewed his pant legs together. Perhaps he will get angry and insist on sewing his own clothes.]

Okay, a little passive-aggressive, admittedly. And not too heavy on the research/footnote side. But I got an A+, the professor laughed as he read it to the class, and it inspired me to take other chances as I continued to write over the years.

Getting back to Mary—by the time she wrote her most major work, *A Vindication of the Rights of Women* (1792) (you *GO,* Mary), she was already fairly well known. The book was as passionate as it was thought-provoking. "It is time," she said, "to effect a revolution to female manners—time to restore them to their lost dignity."

Unfortunately, while she was strong and vocal professionally, Mary had this little problem personally. Let's call it her heart. For as fervent as she was in her writing, she sometimes let that organ get in her way. Of all the kindred feelings I feel for her, my major empathy lies in the addiction that led to her downfall, to 170 years of scorn that plagued her posthumously. Mary, you see, dug men who did not dig her back. And though it went smack in the face of what she proposed in her writing, more than once she succumbed to her desire for blatantly sexist men.

The first one, a married fellow, out and out rejected her. But not before she deified him and convinced herself he would leave his wife. (How long has this foolish way of thinking been going on?) The second one, taking advantage of her isolation as she hid out in France postulating on the French Revolution and watching her friends get their heads lopped off, showed up when he felt like it.

She wrote this guy endless letters in his frequent absences and filled those nights he was around with carnal pleasures. Which led to her first pregnancy. Which led to this dude deciding he wanted nothing to do with her or the kid. Which led him to convince her to take a long vacation, with the baby but without him, to Sweden, Norway, and Denmark. Which led her, feeling lonely, to try to off herself, twice. Hey, at least she failed and lived long enough to write a cool travel guide about the whole thing.

Anyhow, she finally figured things out and got over the guy. But then, because few of us learn our lesson the first time, she fell for yet another man who didn't precisely buy her philosophies. At least he was fairly nice about the whole thing. And when she found herself again pregnant, Godwin—the new guy—married her. Which brought her some happiness. But quite a bit of criticism, too, since she'd spoken out against that institution as oppressive for women.

Fast forward. At the age of thirty-eight, with several books under her belt, Mary Wollstonecraft gave birth to a daughter, also named Mary. The younger Mary would grow up to write *Franken-stein*. Her mother would never see the influence she had on her daughter. Because before that daughter was a week old, Mary Wollstonecraft would die from the complications of childbirth. She could philosophize all she wanted about the societal ills of being a woman in the eighteenth century. Sadly, she could do nothing about the physical ills directly associated with being a woman.

After she died, her husband published an anthology of her works. Included were love letters she'd written him, as well as letters she'd written to the father of her first child. Her husband, in a flash of brilliance, realized it didn't matter that these latter letters were not to him. He saw the passion, the pain, the love. And he wanted to share these with the world.

The world replied with laughter, mockery, condemnation. Wollstonecraft was ridiculed as a slut, a whore, and, in one work (anonymously written, of course), a "usurping bitch." It took over a century and a half more before she was finally re-throned in her rightful role as a righteous babe, hailed as a heroine when the Women's Revolution struck with full-force in the late 1960s and early 1970s.

Some nights, I sit and I write and I wonder what I'm doing. What's the impact, what's the purpose, and how come that boy I had a crush on ten years ago never had a crush back? When I am lucky, for some reason totally beyond me, a purpose presents itself. I get a call of thanks, a note of praise, or stumble back a decade to a writer I'd nearly forgotten.

Pioneer feminists from the 1970s often bemoan the fact that young women these days are losing ground. Because, for example, they have no idea what had to happen just to bring the pay scale up to the current horrendous male/female ratio. Because they laugh at The Revolution and think it was all about burning bras, and don't we all know that WonderBras are better than burnt bras? Because they don't realize how shaky is the ground we walk on, how fast it might crumble beneath us, give way to such sexist patriarchal organizations as the religious right. Because, before any of us know it, if we're not careful, and vocal, we'll be mocked and condemned as usurping bitches. We'll be relegated to some new version of mending and ironing whether we want to or not, waiting to take dictation when the menfolk amble back in the door.

I doubt anyone ever called Dorothy Wordsworth a bitch. The fellows she met through her brother probably thought she was just swell, the way she followed the rules and all, and even offered up her best metaphors for the taking. Me? I'll take the Wollstonecraft treatment any day. Call me what you like, and laugh when my emotions sometimes go directly in the face of my creed.

But know that if I ever have to choose between picking lettuce for a man and, say, taking the guillotine for speaking my mind, no head is better than one.                          (1996)

## SAY DON'T STOP TO PUNK ROCK

In 1976, I was Miss Bicentennial in the Westville, N.J., Fourth of July parade. This claim was not so much title earned as it was designation by default. I had the only mom skilled (or, perhaps, *willing*) enough to darn the requisite ensemble: a high-necked, maxi-length, Betsy Rossish dress with aproned-skirt and matching bonnet (an elasticized, cloth shower cap number).

Looking back, it's hard to fathom that just one year later it was *Good-bye Constitutional Commemoratives and Hello British Invasion Take III*. Never mind the Redcoats and the Mop Tops. This time 'round England's burgeoning punk movement spilled across the big pond with debut records from the Clash, the Jam, and Elvis Costello to name but a few angry young ax-grinders changing the music scene—and, soon enough, my life.

Most memorable, if least talented, was the Sex Pistols. A calculated creation of Malcolm McLaren, they were really just your basic boy band, albeit one that hadn't been to finishing school. They shocked the unsuspecting by using fictitious names like Jonny Rotten and Sid Vicious, ranting and spittling vitriolic lyrics (notably: "I Am the Anti-Christ"), and sporting hairstyles and fashions that made "disheveled" seem a Chanel-tame adjective by comparison.

Some of punk's angst was legitimately political, rooted in the frustrations of London street kids on the dole, furious with a system on the cusp of staunch Thatcherdom. They lashed out with purple, green, or blue Mohawks, startling body piercings, leather-and-stud accessories, shredded pants held together with safety pins, and a steady stream of obscenities.

Lacking proper punk trappings—I was, after all, thirteen, American, and living with my parents, not eighteen, British, and squatting—I couldn't exactly stake full claim to the movement. But sitting in that same bedroom where hung my Betsy Ross dress, listening to Elvis Costello on my eight-track player—*I need my head examined, I need my eyes excited, I'd like to join the party, but I was not invited . . .*—something clicked.

It wasn't until 1983—the year I went away to college—that I hit my true punk pace. I buzzed off my Breck-girl hair, eventually sporting a half-Mohawk and earning a nickname that never went away. I pierced one ear eight times. Best of all, I took up with Brian.

Brian was a strapping six-foot-four-inch skate punk who sang lead vocals for the Impotent Sea Snakes and had a stage name not printable in family periodicals. He turned me on to the New York Dolls, the Specials, the Police (pre-Sting-as-Tantric-jackass). Took me thrift shopping for odd vintage clothes, which I wore when he took me to see purposefully wretched bands screaming in seedy clubs.

I wore Chuck Taylor high-top sneakers (dyed different colors and striped with MagicMarker), took up clove cigarettes, danced hard and crazy, and grew a chip on my shoulder in response to the rude stares and cruel remarks my purposeful external plumage incurred among the mainstream.

I can't say what year I finally lost the energy to maintain the punk aesthetic. But a quarter century after Johnny Rotten spat out, "God Save the Queen," my hair is, once again, Breck straight, long down my back. I wear only three earrings (two of them matching.) And a good percentage of my clothes are Gap-casual, acting as urban camouflage rather than the attention-grabbing styles of my youth.

This hardly means my family was right when they predicted punk was a phase that I would move through, emerging to some other "safe" side. In fact—the joke is on them—the "safe" side now has come to embrace punk.

Because, as retail trips reveal, old punks are today's desired demographic. I head up the spaghetti aisle, I hear Elvis Costello. Move toward the T-shirt rack, greeted by the Go-Gos. Kinko's is especially gratifying with twenty-four-hour piped-in offerings—like some compilation tape carefully mixed for your lover, circa '84.

In truth, these tunes are mostly punk's more poppy cousin, New Wave. Still they can inspire the making of hundreds more copies than intended while waxing nostalgic with the guy two copiers over who also saw the Hooters in Philly back in '83.

Likewise radio stations have caught on, appointing specific programs (e.g. the Flashback Lunch) to revisit these tunes. Listening to these shows is the one time I don't surf during commercials, lest

I miss the beginning of the next set, the opening strains of the Cure, the Talking Heads, the Psychedelic Furs, or A Flock of Seagulls.

Hot Topic, a national chain, is making a killing off of kids like my son, eleven, who loves all the "retro" punk stuff they're selling in a mall, no apologies for the oxymoronic nature of this endeavor. But they get my money because it's the one mall experience I can tolerate for up to twenty minutes at a time, lulled by speakers blaring punk covers by bands whose members weren't even born when the song they're singing was released.

The other day I observed my son with more pride than a preteen aspiring toward pubescent angst probably hopes for from his mom. But I couldn't help myself. His black-and-white hair—he has a stylist regularly provide interesting patterns (polka dots, leopard prints, checkerboard)—was sticking up all over the place. His T-shirt, a recent thrift-store acquisition, read, "The Bush Twins Stole My Beer."

Punk, I was relieved to note, is alive and well—Son of Punk my own legacy of the movement that shaped my world. (2002)

## THE BUMBERSHOOT WALTZ

Sitting parked in front of my vacationing friend's house, committed to caring for her three dogs, I panicked. Outside rain pummeled, lightning struck, thunder rumbled. Not just a rainstorm. Something bigger.

Something big enough to make me suck in my breath, maneuver my way through the small opening between the two front seats, wriggle to the back, and grope around until at last, I extracted it.

Umbrella.

It was a compact number, maybe a foot in length. Tentatively I cracked the door, undid the little snap strap holding it wrapped tight, pushed the tiny button and . . . whoosh . . . it extended, popped open, provided me dry sanctuary the twenty steps to the front door.

Later that night, returning for dinner feeding, my son in tow, I pointed triumphantly to the now flaccid gadget, sitting damp on the porch. (The storm had been as fast moving as it had been harsh—I hadn't needed the umbrella to get back to the car.)

"Look!" I pointed, triumphant.

"Umbrella?" he asked, momentarily puzzled at my excitement.

"I used it!" I said. "Don't you remember?"

"Oh yeah. You're afraid of umbrellas."

I didn't exactly like that he put it that way. It's not like a phobia—some fear that an umbrella gone bad is going to come and kill me in my sleep. Rather it is my Post Traumatic Bumbershoot Incident Disorder that keeps me from using the handy device, except in most dire conditions.

Bumbershoot—that's the nickname they taught us in kindergarten, as we sang the happy rainy day song, "Push UP your bumber-SHOOT!"

Kindergarten. The year it happened. The year of my first umbrella—beloved transparent vinyl, adorned with cheerful green go signs and red stop signs.

I adored it.

So, too, did the stray dog that, one rainy day, burst into the school's mud room and snacked upon the boots and 'shoots therein, destroying my prized possession, leaving some permanent association in my mind. My love affair with umbrellas was short-lived and it was over.

Years later, when I explained this theory to a friend curious as to my avoidance of umbrellas, he asked if I'd considered that I was blaming the victim. Excellent question. Logic dictates that I would not (as I have) grow up to sleep with the enemy. Yet nightly I crawl into the sack with my pack of pooches, though I suppose it would make more sense—comfort notwithstanding—to sleep with a full umbrella stand.

I am hardly the first to have an umbrella aversion. The invention, thought to have been around for at least 4,000 years (appearing in Egypt, Greece, and China—where first it was waterproofed), fell out of fashion for a spell in the Middle Ages.

Then, in 1750, a British traveler brought home an umbrella from a trip to Persia and whipped it out in public. Jonas Hanway—the Brits would begin referring to their umbrellas as Hanways—preferred being dry over being manly, the opinion of the day being that umbrellas were best left to women. This practical attitude brought upon him the wrath of cabbies, concerned that umbrella-enhanced pedestrians would now forgo paying for a ride, preferring to hoof it and save a few pence.

Practicality for the masses won out over disgruntlement of the few. Umbrella popularity grew enough that in 1830 James Smith and Sons, the first all-umbrella shop, opened in England. They moved from Foubert Street to Oxford Street in 1857, and there they remain, 145 years in the same location. No doubt helping along the cause (besides, of course, all that damn rain) was one Samuel Fox, who 150 years ago invented the steel-ribbed umbrella, replacing the more fragile wood frame.

Despite my "fear" of umbrellas, I actually hold them in high regard. I like the way they pop up from nowhere, bursting out of street vendor boxes in on stormy days. I like how tiny they've become, fitting in a purse. And how huge—the "golf" umbrellas soccer parents tote because rain is no reason to stop the game.

I like the designs, the duck handles, the Van Gogh prints. One year, signing up for annual membership at the Missouri Botanical Garden, I chose as my free gift the bright green umbrella printed with plants. My syndrome kept me from using it more than twice, but until I misplaced it, I just loved looking at it, its prettiness bringing me both comfort and a reminder of its source, one of my favorite places in the world.

My friend Sarah had an umbrella like that. Purchased when she was twelve, the year she lived in England. Its pattern was the *London Times*, and she proudly toted it with her when she worked in the newsroom of her college paper.

Once, visiting a friend in San Francisco, I had no choice but to face my fears. It was pouring. A taxi would've taken too long. We had others to meet for dinner. I was handed an umbrella. We were in North Beach, heading into Chinatown.

Chinatown? But it's already impossible to maneuver those streets on a sunny day. What would we do with all those umbrellas? How would we manage? *Somebody might get an eye put out!*

Instead I became part of the Bumbershoot Waltz, a million multi-colored Hanways floating miraculously above the crowds, no one crashing, no one frowning. The rain came down. We did not feel it. Just the glorious rhythm of it drumming upon my own private rooftop. Dry. In the city. In the Rain.                    (2002)

"When you try to analyze it, it just seems so unbelievable. I didn't know a plane could do that much damage." That's Henry Mowgli Gillespie speaking. Fifth grader. Mine.

It's about thirteen hours since the World Trade Towers started collapsing. It's about ten hours since we began watching coverage. I'm not even going to try to make sense of this.

On a typical school day, I drop him off, take my long walk, come home, check the AP wire for news. This day, no time for AP, I've got parent-teacher conference. I'm glancing at email, ready to head to the conference.

Phone rings.

It's Ann. She's crying. Have I heard?

This sentence, I know, means something bad (very) has happened. Without thinking, I log on to a news site as she explains. But the information makes no sense. Does not compute. Impossible.

When you try to analyze it, it just seems so unbelievable.

I listen, but Ann might as well be speaking another language. I get off the phone. I'm going to the conference. Yes I am. That's where I'm going. I'm out the door. The phone rings. I hear it. I run back in.

It's Ross. Have I heard?

I listen, but he is speaking another language, too. I get in the car. I drive to school. As I pull up, the radio informs me . . . wait, what exactly was it? Second plane hit? First tower collapse? I can only remember dropping my head to the steering wheel. Something inside of me is screaming.

Now I walk-run into the building. What if they haven't heard? Creepy nervous excitement—I will break the news! They're safe here, insulated from the outside world. Someone needs to tell them! I make a beeline for the office.

They know. A second grade teacher I pass is calmly guiding kids down the hall. I ask if she's heard. Yes, but she's playing it cool for the kids. Near the office, another second grade teacher is choking up.

I'm stuttering at the principal. What's the plan? Are we closing down? This is unprecedented.

She agrees. Unprecedented. There's a crisis plan but no decision on whether to execute it.

I'm still going to my conference. I'm seizing this concept. Hard. Go to the conference. This might be the last grasp of normal for some time. I tell the principal I'm taking my kid home after the meeting. I call Ann. Can I bring her son, too?

Yes, please.

The conference will be, in its own little way, as surreal as anything else this day. We'll shut the door to the windowless room. Shut the door on the world. No radio. No TV. Just me and the teachers agreeing my son is swell. Talking about improving penmanship. Laughing at the challenges of fifth graders.

The meeting ends. Back in the hall. Back in the office. Sign out the boys. Interrupt the principal, tell her I'm taking Nick, too. Go to the classroom. No kids. Go to the playground. Henry spots me. What, Mom? What are you doing here?

Come with me. Get Nick and come with me.

I can tell they're completely clueless. What, what, what? they want to know.

*Something bad,* I tell them. *I'll explain in the car. Get your things.*

In the stairwell, on the way to gather their things, I start to tell them. They cannot believe this. World Trade Towers are not some foreign concept to them. Nick remembers well admiring them from Ellis Island. And Henry . . .

July 24, 2001: Manhattan. Six weeks ago. Henry and me. Henry's best friend MarkHenry and MarkHenry's dad Ross, my best friend. It's hot as hell and as ever the energy of NYC is stressing me out. I'm here on business, to meet my new agent, Meredith. Ross, so patient, wants to show the boys the sights.

We agree to split up. Ross takes the boys. I head to Rockefeller Plaza to meet with Meredith. Ross and I chat by cell phones. They're at the World Trade Towers. They're in line. It's awesome. They're going up.

In the car more radio. And here is the big thought that goes through my mind: This is it. These boys are changed. From now on it will be *Remember that day we got picked up from school early?*

When it's their generation's turn to answer the question: Do you remember where *you* were? The answer will not be about November 22, 1963. The answer will be about September 11, 2001.

At Ann's I tell her that the principal told me that our friend, Blinda, another school mom, who flies for American, was not in the sky. Now to the big TV.

This is the first I've seen video footage. First not last. Over and over and over and after the first few times Henry will add his own repeating commentary. "Did you see how sharp that plane turned?" Turned. Went into building. Went through building.

Building gone.

We watch. Watch watch watch. We can't not watch. We watch as they zoom in and we see that the falling debris has arms and legs and wears a suit.

The boys build a big fort. Bomb shelter we think. They come out now and then to watch the same footage. To eat the pizza we've bought.

Pizza! The nerve of us! How can we eat at a time like this? How can we not? Nervous consumption. Like laughing at a funeral.

And like laughing at a funeral, we laugh today, too. This is not disrespect. This is disbelief.

Peter Jennings is pretty pulled together. He's organized. He's keeping us calm as he can. I wonder aloud what Dan Rather is doing. I wonder if he's thinking about how they made him stop saying "Courage" at the end of his broadcasts. I wonder if he's thinking, *See, I told you.*

We know Dan can get kooky sometimes, so we switch to him. He doesn't let us down. This is a national emergency. This is, they say, the biggest act of terrorism in the history of the modern world. They show us a tape of the president. The tape fails. Dan Rather to the rescue. "To err is human," he tells us. "But to really foul up you need computers." Or maybe he says "technology." Dan's mind is racing though. You can see it.

The boys pop out of the fort. Yes, they'll remember where they were.

We look for odd-looking commentators, haphazard experts dragged in from thin air, stupid quotes, bad reporting. George Bush, looking like a twelve year old so scared he just shit his pants, keeps saying, "Make no mistake . . ." And I turn to Ann and tell her that he's not supposed to say this out loud, that "make no mistake" is a little flashcard his mommy, Barbara, is holding up for him off screen, trying to prompt him through, keep him from saying something like, "We're gonna get cowboylistic on some Arabs and we will be pit bulls on their pant legs of pugilism, yes sir!" He keeps calling us Merkins. He's going to protect the Merkins. I ask Ann if she knows a Merkin is a pubic wig. (She doesn't.)

We find reasons to giggle. Maybe if we refuse to believe it, maybe Dan Rather will finally crack a smile too. Maybe he'll say, *Aha, folks, I was just kidding, it was all a joke.* It could happen you know—remember Florida last November during the elections.

When you try to analyze it, it just seems so unbelievable.

When I go to pick up the pizza, I stop home to get my knitting. This is my version of smoking since I quit really smoking, which is something I'd very much like to start again right this moment. I think a twisted thought when I think about smoking. I feel pity for anyone in the collapsed building who woke up this morning, vowed it was the first day to quit smoking, never did get to have that last puff before it all went black.

Hey, if the real world can turn surreal on my head, my head can turn surreal in response, right?

I know precisely one stitch: knit. I can make one shape: rectangle. Today I work on a really long rectangle. Used to be I told people who asked I was knitting a cigarette. Today I say I'm knitting a bunker.

I also try to call Meredith. I know she's up there. I know she's midtown. I pray she's midtown. I know a lot of people in New York. I stayed in the fire formerly known as the Millennium Hotel, right in front of the WTC. I can see it all too clearly in my head. All of us are doing this—thinking of who we know up there. Of who we know in Washington. Is Jonathan okay? Are Mitch and Melissa okay?

As we seek connection in happy events, feel the energy surge of joy—parades and weddings and parties and other gatherings—now we seek some connection to this thing we can't believe. Here's the connection: we're all human.

Meredith's phone is busy.

Everybody's phone is busy. I send her an email. Please tell me you're okay, I say.

At Ann's, I call my mom. Mommy. We all want our mommies today. Our mommies and our babies. The boys aren't home because we're worried about their safety so much as we just want them around. The kids and the dogs. Everybody, come here, come close, stick together.

My mom can see Philly from her house just across the Delaware. Thirtieth Street Station is closed, she tells me. My oldest sister, the schoolteacher, is locked down in her school in suburban Jersey. Nobody in, nobody out. They tell the kids recess is off due to some sudden necessary repairs. They don't tell the kids the truth, not yet.

When you try to analyze it, it just seems so unbelievable.

Funny things pop into your head. Henry, a child raised in an era when we are assaulted by media on all sides, wants to know if maybe this is happening to distract attention from Gary Condit. Nick is amazed that George Bush is showing concern for the country. I want to know if anyone else has noticed the date: 9/11. Get it? 911. Emergency.

I am paralyzed, knitting, watching Dan Rather. Later we let Peter Jennings back in. He's got exclusive new footage. Looking up. A plane. Through a building. They can slow it down. Frame by frame.

Somehow, so many hours later, I extract myself, leave Ann's house, wonder—so paranoid now—if it's safe to check my P.O. box. I check. I survive. I don't want to go home. I don't want to cook dinner. I'm exhausted, so exhausted.

We go to the bookstore—I need some research stuff. Really this is just an excuse not to go home. In the store I feel preposterous. How can you be a consumer at a time like this? Henry tells me he's tired, really tired. I tell him trauma will do that.

"Yeah, it sucks the energy right out of you," he says.

We rent a stupid movie because we can't look at the news another second. The movie starts. And zoom in to . . . New York City skyline. I'm glancing away when Henry says look, do I see? See what? I can rewind it, he says, they just showed the World Trade Towers.

He can't rewind it. None of us can rewind it. We are in a stupor. I serve pretzels and Sprite for dinner. Pretzels right from the bag. I can't focus.

He'll turn back into a child at intervals. Without warning he'll slip behind the drum kit and start banging out the song they're learning in school now: "Fifty, nifty United States from thirteen original colonies."

I'll bathe the dogs, do the laundry. I am grasping for normalcy. Now and then he'll look at me. *I can't believe it,* he says. *I wonder how long it took to build that building. It doesn't seem real.*

He's not the only one who can't stop thinking about it. When you try to analyze it, it just seems so unbelievable.   (2001)

# MEN I HAVE NOT SLEPT WITH

*Tell me a story about my dad,* I say.

My older sister, Kitty, bristles. Starts to chastise me. Nothing new. Our cousin Michael, holstered gun hanging at his waist, hushes her. *We're all grown-ups now* he says.

Seated beside me, Uncle Tony smiles. Just a little. He begins. *You know that fireplace stone you had?*

The white slab in front of the gas fireplace. House my parents built. I used it as a desk to teach my baby sister shapes, colors, the letters in her name. It was our runway, too. In church, people saw the eleven of us, front pew, assumed (correctly) the budget was tight. They sent us bags. Clothes funny in their ugliness. Their uselessness, too. Pants with one leg sewn shut. We modeled them up on that stone.

Family portraits feature us kids huddled on it, around it. One year there's six. Then seven. Eight. Nine.

And proms. You couldn't leave until your date stepped up beside you, smiled not at the camera but knowledge of beer in the car.

Until Uncle Tony told me, I never knew the story of the stone.

*See, there was this street in Philly. They were tearing down the houses.*

My dad never understood why anyone threw anything away. Always picked through trash. He took Tony to the street one night to salvage a front step. Stoops they call them in Philly.

Only he couldn't find one he liked. Not at a demolished house. But he did see this one. Okay, so the house was still standing, a light on inside.

*So what? It's a good stone, Tony.*

Tony laughs telling me this. I'm glad. It hasn't been a month since Aunt Barbara died. Sorrow emanates from him like heat from a Texas highway in July.

So my father wants this stoop. Tony's getting nervous. *Then here comes this band of thugs, see?* Heading right for them as my dad pries at this impossible stone. Tony thinks they're dead meat. My father, though, he approaches the guys. Daddy, the human Chihuahua, five-foot eight, convinced he's so much more.

The thugs join in, heft that stone into the car. Soon after, it becomes the centerpiece for our lives.

A few years ago, I called Aunt Barbara. I was getting ready to write about Daddy, expose him for who he was to me. I knew my stories were true. I also knew I'd have hell to pay for telling them.

I wanted reassurance. Other people's proof. My aunt, his only sibling, confirmed, elaborated. Revealed the kind of family stories which make you wonder, after awhile, why you went digging in the first place. Told how badly she'd wanted to be more a part of our lives. He said no.

Tony got on the phone, too. Ever the peacemaker, he always danced lightly around the topic of my father. He kept his commentary brief.

*You did the right thing. You got out.*

Daddy always said she was crazy, talked too much. We believed him the way little kids must.

Aunt Barbara. Perfect hair. Frosted lips. Perfume. Like a movie star.

My grandmother lived with my aunt and uncle. My father visited her nearly every night before he took the bridge back over to the Jersey side, after another long day in the Pennsylvania rail yards. Uncle Tony told me something else. Sometimes when he left, Mom-mom walked around, muttering to herself. *He's going to go home and make her pregnant again*, she'd worry, aloud, for my mother.

Kitty winces at this. She's mad, I think, that I'm pressing for more. But she's fascinated, too. I'm being naughty again. My official family job. Swing by every few years, fulfill my duties, retreat into the sunset.

Tell me about the funeral, about the accident. He tells me. He cries. It was awful.

A few years ago he had a stroke or two. She took care of him every day. I look at the collage, assembled for the funeral. Dark Italian Tony. Movie-star Barbara. Tony and Barbara—they were a pair.

Once in a while we visited their row house, sat on the plastic-covered couch. In the basement stood Tony's drum kit. Behind it a picture of his hero, Gene Krupa, wailing on the skins. My cousins took turns pinning me to the basement floor, making me mad, like cousins do, all forgotten, forgiven, going back across the Delaware.

Times they'd come our way, we couldn't wait for Uncle Tony to sit down, light a smoke, and start. Spooky stories. Dusk falling on a summer night, glowing cigarette ember the eyes of the monsters he invented to scare us.

Now Kitty and I listen as the stories swirl away from the accident and Daddy, drift toward the otherworldly. They moved to our town once, I guess so my grandmother could be closer to my dad. They left quickly though. Tony explains.

*There were these ghosts. One played the banjo late at night.* They all heard it. *Moved the refrigerator, too.* Listening, I'm ten again, skin crawling.

I never saw her after that phone call.

Last February. Sunday morning. Marathoners run past my house. My son hands paper cups of sports drinks to exhausted runners. I'm sitting by idly, in my pajamas and robe, drinking a latte, having a smoke.

I go inside. There's a message. My sister Mare. *Call home right away*, she says. I hear forced calm like a horse smells danger. I know. In the five seconds it takes to dial, and the five other seconds it takes to connect, I wonder, *Who is it? Mom? Dad? One of the kids?* Stomach twists.

*Aunt Barbara*, she says. *Hit by a truck.* I go blank. Disconnect. Decide I am cold and horrid for feeling so little.

It won't register for another week or so. I'll be out at a movie with a friend. *Miracle at Morgan Creek*, by Preston Sturgis. Old Hollywood comedy. The dad character is mean and yells at his daughters. The rest of the audience laughs, hysterical.

Ha. Ha. Ha.

I just want to weep.

A single line of dialogue triggers a memory. Suddenly, I need to buy Cheap Trick's *Live at Budokan*. The first record I ever bought. I am crossing the bridge back now, over the river time, back to his house.

Driving home, she comes to me and I start to cry. In the house, I blast "Surrender" over and over. I am so damn angry at my father.

She always sent gifts, no matter how much he shooed her away. Avon lotions. Trinkets. The magnet still on my refrigerator, shaped like a Christmas tree ball. Bright. Shiny. Reflecting back a distorted view.

Tony points to the fireplace before we go. *One hundred and seventy-four,* he says. That's how many bricks there are. He's been counting them ever since she died. If he counts those bricks one more time . . . he says.

I'm back in Texas. Mare calls again. That's her family job. Tony gave up she says. OD'ed.

But they saved him.

He lives with my cousin Michael now. He misses Bobbi. That's what he called her. God he misses her. But he doesn't miss those bricks. (2000)


## ROBERT

I'm standing at the kitchen sink, head under running faucet. Robert is washing my hair. He is massaging my scalp and I am whining, as I have countless times before, bemoaning another breakup. "What's wrong with me?"

I can't remember how, during this whimpery rant, I work a certain fact into this conversation. But I do, my voice echoing off the sides of the basin.

Robert, ever dramatic, upon hearing said detail steps back, nay, *recoils.*

"He *what?*" intones my friend in that deep voice he uses to make a living doing radio ads. "You didn't tell me *that.*"

"Did too." By now my other assembled friends, sitting at the table, are focusing on bladder control as they laugh uproariously.

"I tell her—do not get eenvolved wis zee man who believes in chastity belts!" says Frenchy, exhaling a long stream of smoke.

Okay, so it's true. I dated a king from the SCA. The Society for Creative Anachronism. Those folks who dress up in medieval costumes and who, as my friends indelicately put it, beat each other with aluminum-foil-covered Wiffle ball bats on the weekends.

"He wears a *dress?*" asks Robert, incredulous.

This puts me in a peculiar position. I'm really upset with the king. I invested time and money traveling to spend a very long, very crappy week with him. Yet Robert's criticism puts me on the defensive. I feel like I have to stick up for the guy—stick up once again for what we all know, and have known for many years, is my incredibly awful taste in men.

"Not *dresses*," I explain. "*Tunics*. He sews them himself."

Frenchy needs a hanky. Her eyes are leaking something fierce.

Before the afternoon is over, Robert, to put a fine point on his disgust with those who would re-create such a dark time in history, will dance on the edge of political correctness. He will tell us, no really, he understands—in fact *he* likes to play "Plantation" on the weekends.

Okay, Robert, point taken.

And I'm sorry to keep putting my friends through this, but the truth is: I, Spike, have a long history with geeks and freaks. That's my "type."

Give me a bespectacled ninety-eight-pound weakling with a huge, throbbing brain—excellent. Give me an oddball who premasticates tuna filets for his cats—that's okay, too. A man in a dress who fancies himself royal? Might as well give it a shot.

But I have learned, the hard way, that I must draw the line somewhere. Must quit making excuses for guys whose behavior makes me squirm. Did I really enjoy that afternoon in the park, His Highness irked with me for not being impressed when lowly serfs in funny metal hats knelt before him to plead he wallop them with a shiny Wiffle ball bat?

Okay, I did not. That should have been a clue: listen to your gut. No. I am a slow learner. I needed *more* lessons.

A new man materialized. Oddly, like his royal predecessor, he stood six-foot-five, sported long hair, radiated arrogance.

"You aren't in the SCA are you?" I asked, nervous to hear his response.

No. But he thought it was neat. And he did play fantasy games on the weekend. And he was real interested in Vulcans.

I should've run, right then. Instead, I stayed. Nearly a year. The whole affair and consequential breakup like an ancient moat's bridge—long, drawn out, and utterly warped.

Not long after I managed to escape him, who can say why, I

watched *Star Trek* one night. Had never seen it before—ever—though my ex never missed an episode, could not spend one Saturday night with me due to a standing date with his geek roommates to traverse the final frontier via the tube.

Stunned, I listened to the dialogue, realizing he had never spoken an original line to me—everything he ever needed to know he learned on the *Enterprise*.

I remembered then what Robert asked me, another day in the kitchen, when I had first enthusiastically described Trekkie-boy to him.

"Why is it that whenever you meet a new man, the same song runs through my mind?" he mused.

With that, he began humming a circus theme.          (2000)

## ROSS

From the yoga studio, I call Ross on his cell phone, thankful that he answers.

"Where are you?" I ask.

"Party Pig."

I'm not surprised. In the past week, between us we've logged a decent amount of time at the Pig.

"Well, when you're done, can you run over to my house? I'm pretty sure I turned the eyeballs off but I'm not positive."

It's not the first bizarre exchange we've had this week. Certainly it won't be the last. We'll continue to touch base often throughout the days and nights leading up to the Halloween carnival at our sons' school. For the third year running, our job is to transform the cafeteria into a Haunted House.

That first year, Sarah, the carnival chair, loved to brag, half-jestful (half-not) how she had recruited the "tattooed and gay parents" into the carnival fold. Tattooed and gay, that's me and Ross respectively. Cliché dictates that by virtue of our "abnormalcy" we should be questionable parents, certainly not the extracurricular sort. But there we are, pitching in at various extracurricular events, stealing the show annually in late October.

Not to say we're completely cliché-free. Ross is prone to a perennial case of what I term Gay Halloween Vanity, where he determines that he and he alone will have the most elaborate, well-thought-out, stunning costume. I don't even attempt to match him in that department.

In fact, Ross's main job for this event is to be the supplier of enthusiasm. My job is to complain constantly, tell him over and over this is the last year, all this grumbling offered while I simultaneously fashion beer flats into tombstones, supervise fourth graders wielding spray paint, boil spaghetti (to be mixed with dye and jello for brains), boil eggs (to be mixed with dye and sliced into eyeballs), slice bananas (to be mixed with dye for amputated fingers), halved red peppers (to be filled with jello for hearts).

That first year was particularly challenging. I was dating the guy who was going to be our vampire. We were arguing constantly. Sarah begged me not to break up with him until he'd fulfilled his duties. On top of this, I was on a new (wrong) medication to combat depression, pharmaceuticals that left me jittery and out of it. My witch costume—a sheer black dress over my bathing suit, chosen in part to offend the principal—shocked even me when the zipper up the front broke leaving me more Elvira-esque than even I was comfortable with. Vampire boy showed up late and left early, but not before flipping off some little kid who informed him, "You make a lousy vampire."

Through all this, Ross held the show—and me—together. Ross is like that. He'll sit with you through your months-long divorce, watch every Bette Davis and Joan Crawford movie ever made, and let you cry and tell the same story over and over again. He'll tell you not to worry about the vampire, that soon enough a more polite werewolf is bound to come along.

Year two was somewhat uneventful. I was a much calmer, depression- and vampire-free, low-key devil with glowing horns. Ross, in a mummy costume that took more than an hour to apply, had to eventually be cut out so he could pee.

I swore this year would be our last. He told me to relax—it was going to be a blast. He sent me to the fabric store for certain items to create a mystery costume which he refused to describe to me.

"I think I need seven yards of this and two yards of this," I told the fabric cutter. "But I'm not sure." She looked at me funny.

At the thrift store, shopping for props and costumes for the teens who'd volunteered to play ghouls, I was amused to find some of my own recently donated clothes on the rack designated "Halloween."

The big day arrived. More phone exchanges. At two-thirty P.M., three hours before show-time, I made a point to Ross.

"Every year, when I'm wiped out and high from the excitement of it all, right afterwards, you convince me to do it again. Well I am here to point out to you this year, before we begin, while we're both exhausted, that we are not doing it again."

Ross, who'd been up 'til five A.M. that morning working on his costume, begged to differ. Mid-conversation I swore. "What?" he asked. "I forgot to make the Jack-o-lanterns."

What good is the cemetery without Jack-o-lanterns? I raced to school, picked up our sons and another volunteer, raced to the HEB, bought pumpkins and other last minute supplies, raced home, carved the pumpkins, loaded the car, and got to the school by four.

He was already there, enthusiastic friends in tow, all of them transforming away. In ninety minutes the cafeteria was a scary place. While I supervised the finishing touches, Ross disappeared to put on the mystery costume. I had already put on my slapped together mish-mash. (I told you, there's no competing with Ross.) All evening the kids would say to me, sometimes in a bratty sneer, "What are you supposed to be?"

"Why I'm the elephant-nosed troll woman with striped legs," I'd reply, from under my trunk, pulling up my tutu to reveal my fashion tights, then stroking my fluorescent pink troll wig. "Haven't you seen my show on Saturday mornings?"

They didn't laugh.

Ross, it turned out, had built himself a costume that made it appear as if he were a torso-less head, being held up by an eight-foot tall man.

For nearly three hours I'd lead groups of children through the haunted house, my ghouls turning their performance up or down, depending on whether I announced, "We have a bunch of little ones," or "We have a group of skeptical teenagers here . . . "

We'd go past the devil, the witches, the cemetery, Franken-stein, the food table (featuring a real human head poking up through a roasting pan). Past the coffin, past our friend Danny huddled into his black costume, waiting 'til the last minute to jump out.

And there, at the end of the line, Ross.

"Have you seen my body?" he asked the shrieking kids. Or sometimes he'd stand silent, waiting for them to approach, to debate if he were real or just a statue.

My rubber elephant trunk filled with the condensation of me, dripped sweat out the nostrils. My rubber elf shoes grew coated in a nasty layer of jello and the Rice Krispies we'd scattered around the floor for creepy crunchy effect. Round and round I went, and each time I passed Ross, Mister Enthusiasm, I burst out laughing in spite of all prior complaints on my part.

Already he's planning for next year. And, he informs me, I'm a part of that plan. Scary. (2000)

## BOB

A rooster rustles in my neighbor's garden. I laugh and think of Bob.

Bob's full name is Robert Vivian. Jot it down because I am going to explain now why you stand to benefit from his collection of essays, *Cold Snap as Yearning*.

For now, though, let's just call him Bob.

Bob is a rare bird, rarer than an urban rooster. I like to think him a kindred spirit, though maybe we should crank that up a notch. Because some days Bob hovers up there in the realm of angels (angels who, mind you, sport devilish grins).

It's last March. My beloved buddy John, a.k.a. John the Baptist (JTB for short), calls. Spring break is coming and JTB, a doctoral candidate at the University of Nebraska, is thinking Austin might be a sight warmer than Lincoln right then. Might he visit and bring his friend Bob? Sure, I say, come on down.

I suppose my deep love of real-life drama causes me to choose the evening of their arrival (specific time unknown) for a poop-or-get-off-the-pot chat with a young man who has been acting maybe interested in me. Tired of mixed messages, I invite "Ricky" over for The Talk.

It really is a dark and stormy night. Ricky and I are making awkward progress, teetering toward cusp of kiss or cuss (who can guess?) whence comes upon the door a knock. Deus ex machina, they call it in theater. John and Bob, we call it at my house. A sudden, out-of-the-blue (well, almost) conclusion to the drama at hand.

With all due respect to Ricky, who isn't really a bad man (but certainly not the right man), JTB and Bob do me an enormous favor. By the time the two of them are done doting on me, reminding me of the shape and smell and sound of true respect, the aforementioned potential fling is flung. Right out the door.

A new me—or, more aptly, a reawakened old me—emerges.

I have always loved words. The rhythm. The power. The beauty. The strength.

Oh, yes, and the cash. No excuses, more than a few hack pieces have borne my byline: teen-mag articles, shopping tips, product descriptions.

Essays, novels, memoirs, columns, poetry—this work sustains my soul. But when you get down to the dirty business of big bucks, it's the commercial avenue one must drive down should one regularly desire luxuries: food, gas, lodging.

Still, despite my heap o' hack, I never forget epiphanic moments gathered earning my lit degree. Metaphysical poetry. Postmodern beauty. Russian prose. Too often, sidetracked by life's rush, I relegate these things, dusty, to the bottom shelf of time.

Enter John. Enter Bob. They are studying to become English professors who will astonish with classics the hearts of new batches of the unlearned and eager. Talking with them, I vividly recall the one love that never failed me, never sent mixed signals, never strung me along or made me wait.

I'm not talking about cigarettes.

Together, the three of us commit acts for which, should some nonliterary soul happen by, surely we would be mocked in our geekishness. *Look at them! Reading poetry—aloud! Reading plays. Discussing authors. Confessing favorite writing techniques.*

We are writers. And, I guess, a little nutty in our habits, our reclusive states. To me, what is funny about writing is, so often writers prefer to be alone to create work we hope will connect with masses. Help me, professors: Is this irony?

One day, during the visit, we are porching (aside: with my

poet's license I've coined this verb), enjoying the jungle green of spring. A stranger pops by, points. "Is that your stray rooster?"

Uh, no. Nor do we know a single blessed thing about roosters. (Something we unexpectedly discover as we try to determine how best to wrangle the rooster back to safety behind the garden gate of my absent neighbor. Our greatest collective tool—words—sway not the bird. Not even *please*.)

Ask any of us to describe this moment; receive varied accounts. My pivotal moment is a look on Bob's face: *A rooster?* And then: *Of course—a rooster!*

Bob does amazing things. Because he has an odd quiet, only after he departs will it occur to me that he is a character I could not create, not even in my best fiction.

Nonchalantly he walks across my hardwoods. On his hands. Unhesitant he recites a translation of the Polish poet Czeslaw Milosz's gorgeous *On Angels*. (This he does, somehow sans pretense, outside at a bar, in the rain, while Ricky's rock band wails onstage.)

For breakfast, he serves the children an odd poem about a fork. Delighted, they beg to hear it again at dinner. Children begging for poetry at supper? *What next? More liver, please?*

In his trunk: an 8 x 10 glossy of his ex-wife, Kay. He is hardpressed to capture his ongoing deep love for her despite his boundless gift of words. (*I wish you could meet her,* he sighs.) Oh, there's a bullwhip, too. Wait, don't worry, it's a prop.

Bob writes plays. Did he forget to mention this? Twenty-two works produced in New York. And a book coming soon, too.

An advance copy arrives. I read the pieces, one per night, as if this collection is the last box of chocolates ever. I read carefully—to enjoy his style, yes, but to see where we are the same and where we are not, too.

This is not a competition, I know, but come on—into every writerly relationship a little comparison must fall. The differences I spot easily.

Spike loves careening through the language, as if on a list-free shopping spree at Target. Bob (writing motto: *Speed Kills*) seems to have spent life's stolen moments exploring the hallways of the Oxford English Dictionary, probing, memorizing exact words to fit precise and scenic inner landscapes.

He finds beauty in details and details in everything and everyone: street people, trash pickers, ancient women. Shopping carts, death, the drive to his graveyard shift at UPS. Insurance claims, childhood pranks, the Nebraska sky.

He knows well intimate places—in memory, in the heart, in imagination, and along that horizontal space on the inside of your wrist, between mitten and jacket sleeve, that grows red and chapped when the snow melts into it. These are places we all know but forget we know. Because we haven't been there in forever. Because we are there all the time.

Reading Bob, I am a newborn, eyes rolling back, the ecstasy of latching on. Simple, powerful, innate response, the sort that comes only with immediate, deep connection: *Ahhhh! Nourishment!* and *I am full with this!*

Milosz says: *The voice—no doubt it is a valid proof, as it can belong only to radiant creatures.*

It is Bob's radiant voice in my mind that comforts me at certain times, when no other voice will do. This is why I have come to call him Bob Hope.

Parting ways, I am reluctant to leave his presence. Yet I find comfort at the source, Bob himself, who has taught me, with his words, that it is necessary to move forward but without worry because, he promises: *Whatever I love is with me always.*    (2001)

## MISTER HAYASHI

A couple of days into our Japan trip, Henry and I are still pretty jetlagged. But exhaustion is just one component of the daze that blankets us. For weeks preceding our first trek abroad, we try to guess how wild it will be to immerse ourselves in a foreign culture.

Despite most vivid imaginations, we could not prophesize what the Far East would do, beyond guessing—correctly—that it would change our lives. For good. For better.

Everywhere we look something piques, astounds, or (most often) both. Kiyomi and Junko, our friends and mother-daughter hostesses, try to accommodate the rat-a-tat questions as we fire them. Tell us about this vending machine, that shrine, the history of Samurai, the words on that sign.

The process is complicated and spellbinding—Junko translates our questions into Japanese for her mother, the two consult, Kiyomi replies in Japanese, and then Junko takes this answer, coupled with her own thoughts, and translates them back for us.

Beyond these conversations, I will not hear flowing, constant English for two weeks. The rhythm of this foreign language, and the very language itself—at once surrounds me and yet is so beyond comprehension that it becomes a meditative chant. I ride upon sound waves I cannot extract literal meaning from, my thoughts swirling, thick bright brush strokes over this audio canvas.

Japan's magic amplifies.

On this day, we are to meet Mister Kiyoshi Hayashi, family friend and younger brother of Junko and Kiyomi's next door neighbor back in Kita Kamakura, where they live in a big house on a mountain. We take the train north to Tokyo.

We spot each other simultaneously. I smile, wonder if he has dressed especially for us—he is wearing a cowboy hat with a rose in its band. We greet each other with enthusiastic bows.

"Konnichiwa!"

"Konnichiwa!"

Mister Hayashi is the Japanese Santa Claus. Like his counterpart, he wears red and white. In lieu of North Pole snow, fallen cherry blossom petals swirl around him to the ground. He begins doling out gifts from his sack.

Henry receives a disposable camera. We're going to the zoo and Mister Hayashi knows a child must be able to capture wild animals on such occasions. For me he has maps of Tokyo, old and new.

Midday, weary legs and hunger coax us to a picnic area where Mister Hayashi produces lunch from that bottomless bag. He hands us famous-brand box lunches—compartmentalized meals, gourmet Lunchables, if you will. These include rice, pickled baby eggplant, radish, snow peas, some shiny whole sardines, pieces of fish. Junko exclaims how jealous her brother Makoto—my friend back in Texas, the reason I have found these wonderful people—will be when he hears what I've eaten.

I watch Henry's face register this food before him, observe him play with it, push it around, feign thrill and gratitude. But

Mister Hayashi sees you when you're sleeping, knows when you're awake. Certainly he recognizes fear of fish when he sees it.

Over both my protests and my son's, Mister Hayashi buys Henry French fries, which the relieved and grateful child proceeds to eat with hashi (chopsticks) to the amusement of us all. I unwittingly return the favor of entertainment when, mid-bite, I am informed that my "fish," something I love, is actually eel, something I have a major mental block about eating. Henry's thought-bubble, invisible to all but me, reads triumphant: "Touché!"

In fact, if I don't think about it, the eel is actually pretty good. And Santa Hayashi garnishes the meal with stories told in English broken poetically. My favorite is a philosophy of old Tokyo, known as "iki."

The closest I can come to translation is something akin to Shakespeare's line about eating, drinking, and being merry, seeing as mañana, we're gonna kick it. Apparently there were some hardcore Tokyo dudes back in the day who liked to stay out all night, get wild, push the envelope, and not go home until they'd spent every last dime. Finally: instant resonance on my part, no further translation necessary.

To better illustrate iki, Mr. Hayashi reaches in his pocket and pulls out a roll of five hundred yen coins—golden shiny, solid heavy. He hands us each the rough equivalent of a hundred bucks and tells us, "You must spend this tonight."

I feel like I did when my grandmother used to pull us aside, slip us dollar bills, admonish us to hush—thus overruling my mother's earlier-in-the-day imperative that we mustn't take from her.

Somehow it comes to light that Mister Hayashi was born the day after my mother, same year. I do the math, calculate the time change over so many zones, realize the amazing. Odds are high they were born within hours, perhaps minutes of each other. The way this man so instantly cares for us, I am not one bit surprised.

Next he hands us envelopes decorated with the characters for *big* and *income*. We inscribe the date and our initials. Soon, he says, we will go to the temple of the God of Wind and Thunder where we will fill these envelopes with incense smoke, then seal them to insure a wealth of health and money and blessings.

Somewhere in the throes of this adventure, Mister Hayashi gives us more gifts still. For me there will be gorgeous prints of Japanese art. For Henry, the loan of a little booklet bulging with stamps. These aren't just any stamps either. They all come from the same source—love letters from the woman who broke our kind friend's heart. It is a description offered straight on, but now, if you look close, can you see it? Is that sorrow in the back of his eyes?

Another night, back on the mountain in Kamakura, Henry and I will gently spread all these stamps out—bright collage of unrequited love—on a blanket on the floor. We'll awe at the sheer quantity before us, scrutinize the details of the art, ponder who this mystery woman was, wonder where she's gone.

But first, there is dinner, Tokyo finale. Mister Hayashi ushers us to a cacophonous sushi bar, where Henry—because he both craves sleep and does not crave any more fishy run-ins—puts his head down on the bar and sleeps. The conveyor belt of raw sea delicacies resting on rice floats by, Japanese sugarplums dancing in his head.

Kiyomi gestures and exclaims when the Sumo wrestlers enter. The "smaller" one gladly poses for a picture with us. I am too amazed and amused to think, for now, how this seems like some preposterous film we are in, directed by Mister Hayashi, who will eventually be revealed as some distant Asian cousin of Frank Capra.

Ever-thoughtful, Mister Hayashi makes one last stop, a hamburger for Henry, before he puts us back on the train. He sends us off in high iki fashion—the more costly Green Car, guaranteed plush seats where we drop off into the sort of sleep where we can't be sure this wasn't all a dream. (2001)

## NEIL DIAMOND AND ME

Everyday, he is with me, watching me type. My muse.

Neil Diamond.

Poster on the wall. Patron saint of fitting big thoughts in small spaces using limited words.

The first time Neil comes into my life I am a kid in a house full of kids expected to be silent the minute Daddy walks in from another long hard day. Sunday nights are worst, the one night we eat en masse, eleven of us at that Last Supper table he built, lined up wordless on vinyl covered benches.

*Please God don't let me be the one to spill my drink or make a snorting noise when my sister makes a face at me across the table.*

His wrath. His glare. The ever-present threat of that black leather belt.

While I am hard-pressed to think up a less happy person, odd exceptions to his steady misery dot our lives the way you might find a bite or two worth salvaging in a burnt pizza pie.

He hates the neighbors. He loves the beach. He is painfully, vocally, racist. He loves old cars. He makes me feel stupid and worthless and rejected. He loves to make dramatic statements.

Like the old airport limousine he buys—paints *Proud Mary* across the front, our names along the four doors on either side, and *ABORTION IS KILLING YOUR OWN CHILD*, splashed huge across the back.

Paydays, he takes his meager trucker salary, buys fruit and bread at the Italian market over in Philly, and flowers for my mom before handing her what's left to get us through on ten-cent bread and fatty beef.

He buys records, too. 45s. No matter how tight the budget, Daddy brings us pop. I twirl to Simon and Garfunkel's "59th Street Bridge Song (Feeling Groovy)." Learn B-sides to the Carpenters hits. Beatles. Mamas and the Papas. And, of course, Neil Diamond.

Daddy spends lots of time in the basement, filled with the accoutrements of dad-ness: pool table, bar (though he rarely drinks), curling-cornered photos from the Korean War. A gold-lamé bikini-ed Barbie captured in a birdcage.

And the stereo. Up from the closed trapdoor that seals him safely away from us emanates *Jesus Christ Superstar* in the '70s. Gloria Gaynor, the Village People, Donna Summer—toot, toot, hey, beep, beep—take over in the '80s.

I don't think my uber-Catholic father ever picked up on the lyrics' drug and homosexual references during this disco stage. I think—really—he just dug the music.

There are instruments, too. Cheap little guitars with nylon

strings, a huge accordion, clarinet, drum kit, trumpet, saxophone. An untuned upright piano that he "plays by ear"—nameless tunes that are often tuneless, too. He could sit there for hours.

I learn one set of scales on the piano. Get pretty good at sax, dabble in clarinet. On guitar, Johnny Cash's "I Walk the Line" is my first song. One of Daddy's favorites.

I will learn his language.

One time, when I am thirteen, he hears about a songwriting contest to honor the sainting of Philadelphia's Bishop John Neumann. Daddy can't read or write music. Painstakingly he creates a melody to accompany simple words. He plunks it out, repeatedly, slowly, while I, seated beside him, do my best to figure out where to draw the notes on the blank music sheets. I don't know if it occurs to him that serious professionals will be our competition.

We can never win.

By eighth grade, I give up instruments for failed attempts at sports and boys. At eighteen, I leave home, leave him. The music stays with me. I seek it always. As punk rocker. As lead singer's girl. As groupie dancing dancing dancing crazy, sometimes all alone.

Six years and a thousand miles later, I hear it on the radio one day:

I am, I said,
To no one there.
And no one heard at all,
*Not even the chair.*

Neil Diamond.

His next concert, I take money I don't have, buy tickets I can't afford under the guise of taking my man as a joke. But I'm hooked by the second song. That night, we buy a poster. The next year we have a baby. Two years later, we break up.

I get the poster. And the baby.

The baby grows up pretty quick and very smart. Last Christmas, he hands me a big box. I open it. Neil Diamond tickets.

I burst out crying.

At the show I am close enough to the stage that I can throw

some intimate apparel and easily land it on Neil's head. I don't. Neil is older now, his pants are higher-waisted. I'm thinking next tour he'll be ordering up some Sans-a-belt slacks from *Parade* magazine.

But still—Mr. Diamond sparkles.

I catch myself fighting a tear when he starts singing about how the radio played in the other room:

*Can you hear it, babe?*
From another time
From another place
Do you remember it, babe?

I am momentarily gutted like we're alone in this room and this isn't the 600,000th time he's sung this tune. Like it's wafting up through the trapdoor, straight into my ears.

I have argued often with sundry siblings over the need or not to forgive our father—now old and feeble, smaller than me, so very much smaller than I used to think he was, when he ruled me with his terror and rage. I point out if I were married to a man who treated me as my father has, they would beg me to escape. I say life is not a TV movie, with a stupid happy ending around every corner. I note that it's not like there's some good old relationship waiting to be repaired.

No. I was a thorn. He made that clear.

Not until I cut off that voice—his voice—could I begin to heal. It is a flawed healing, a voice I can never fully silence. It is Sisyphean, this battle to remember that a demanding father's imperatives are ever-changing, thus never met.

And yet, I think . . .

Despite my son's father's absence, the task of single parenting has been made much less difficult because I can tell the child, honestly, how much I love his father, how much his father loves him. Great advice I picked up years ago from one of the Van Buren/ Landers sisters—never insult your child's other parent, for you insult half the child then.

I have hated my father. And so I have hated myself. With time as water over anger's stone, the edges smooth, though the rock remains hard. Cracks come rarely, courtesy of glimpses of my father, shining momentarily like a sequin on Neil's shirt, some crazy fleeting memory of a happy moment when he was almost nice.

Mostly, these moments come through music. Favorites of his that have become favorites of mine. My own obsession with seeking out the best music. My need to pass this on.

Every night, I sing to Henry, "Everything's Alright," a song from *Jesus Christ Superstar*, the same music my father used to escape me. Neil Diamond watches from the wall in the other room, a curious symbol of his parents' love, the very thing that made him.                                    (2002)


## FRED

In the house where I grew up, in the garage-turned-rec-room, stood one of the many oddities my father was always salvaging from God knows where. This find was an old-style phone booth that stood, like some vertical coffin, three sides wood, one side folding glass door, with a little bench inside. It was a favored perch of my teenage sisters, who sought the privacy it availed in a house with many rooms but few doors.

I was twelve in the fall of 1976, my first year at the junior/senior high school where my sisters, Mare and Kit, were a senior and junior respectively, too busy being Real Teenagers to be bothered with me.

Mare, sweet elfin jock magnet, attracted strapping young athletes with peach fuzz and shy grins, perfect fodder for the false hopeful dreams of this scrawny seventh grader still waiting for my first period, my first kiss, my life to begin.

Fred was my favorite. Six-foot-three. Dreamy eyes. Wavy hair. Even better than his aesthetic gifts was the fact that he took the time to speak to me when he called, as if he had called for me, not Mare, as if he wasn't in any hurry at all, not one bit. As if seventh graders were infinitely interesting to senior boys. Me, in the phone booth, being quizzed on how my life was by Fred.

God I loved him.

Number 73—his football jersey number. Whenever I see that

number, regardless of context (TV channel, price tag, random appearance on a license plate), immediately I think of Fred.

Fridays, seventh period, are reserved for pep rallies out at the football field. I am in the marching band, sectioned off from the stoners and the jocks and the geeks, our own special brand of weird.

One Friday, it is decided that the most popular football players will emerge dressed as nursery rhyme characters. Fred sports a green dress with white polka dots. Maybe he's Lil Bo Peep.

Really it doesn't matter, this is drag before *Tootsie*, before drag is a common thing. Collectively we die of laughter, cheerleaders jump and shout, and I pick up my saxophone to bleat out some peppy, off-key something with the rest of the band.

And now our temporary drag queens, our Most Popular Guys in the Entire School, hit the stands to pick one person each to be their Most Special Personal Fan at Saturday's game.

My hair is greasy and long enough to hide behind, which I do, simultaneously wishing hard to be picked and chastising myself for being stupid enough to wish at all. He'll never pick me.

He picks me.

I follow him down the bleachers, to the track, mortified with joy. Standing next to him towering over me, the crowd cheering, I fold into myself, a nervous wreck, stunned, elated, unworthy, overjoyed.

He picked me!

Spring comes, Mare and Fred graduate, break up, Mare starts dating Johnny.

A year passes. I come home from school one day. Behind my father's ominous hedgerow lie my mother's gifts: Roses the red of cartoon blood ramble up trellises. Azaleas, never subtle, shout hello. Purple Rose of Sharon bursting by the front step. A Japanese red maple, deep in thought. Bright bedded flowers circle concrete Virgin Mary in a half shell.

In the green grass sits Mare. Quiet.

I go inside. I'm standing before the big round mirror, combing my hair, telling a joke. I even remember the joke. Am I telling it to my mother? I think so. I think she's the one who stops me mid-joke, tells me.

Fred. Dead. Car wreck.

My parents won't let me go to the memorial, tell me I'm too young. I spew and rant over the unfairness of this but have no choice. Mare goes, I stay home and think of Fred. Cry.

In the hallways at school I glance sideways at his younger brother, making out with his girlfriend against the lockers. He's a couple of years older than me. We never talk. He graduates. I graduate. We move on.

Three years ago, on a visit, I stay with Mare and Johnny and their four kids. They now live in the town where Fred grew up. I go for a long walk, come back, describe a house I passed. I know I've never been in this house. But for some reason I know it.

"Fred's house?" I ask Mare.

My memory, eerie in its unrelenting way, astounds my sister yet again. Fred's family hasn't lived there in forever. But someone must've once pointed it out to me. It is an outstanding house, very Edward Gorey gothic, tall, imposing. Unforgettable.

Like my Fred. Twenty-five years since that pep rally now. The length of his life and then some and still, I need not photograph nor verbal cue to conjure him. Taking the time. Picking me.

(2002)

TEXAS

## THE DABBS HOTEL

Three old, black cast-iron skillets sit sizzle-hot on the cutting board that protects the flowered vinyl table cloth that covers the long table—one of two, end-to-end, extending the length of the bright blue dining room, and flanked by plank benches.

Skillet one: chunky cut potatoes and onions, crisp brown. Skillet two: top secret drop-dead delicious gravy (recommended on the spuds). And finally, skillet three: possibly the best biscuits in Texas, cut lovingly with the open end of a jelly-jar tumbler, all huddled in a heated circle, awaiting their momentary fork-filled fate.

This is breakfast at the Dabbs Railroad Hotel in Llano, Texas. Prepared by Gary Smith, proprietor, resident innkeeper, head chef, and storyteller extraordinaire. It's the sort of food you eat fast because you can't stop yourself and then, when you are absolutely full to the point another bite will mean death-by-bursting, you put your fork down, get up from the table, walk over to the skillets and git some more.

Llano, Texas, is roughly eighty miles northwest of Austin, right about where east/west Highways 71 and 29 dovetail and intersect with north/south Highway 16. The Dabbs sits on the west bank of the Llano River, and to reach it, you sort of just have to know to turn right, into "that dirt area," just on the west side of the bridge.

That might sound hard to find, but you know, it's not—not really. And certainly not as hard to find as it was when Smith stumbled upon the place, overrun with weeds, back in 1987.

Though Smith, a native of Mason (up the holler 'bout thirty miles and home to Fort Mason, one-time edge of the Texas frontier), once stayed in the hotel in the '60s, enough time had marched on by '87 that the place had long since shut down. Most everyone forgot about it except whoever was responsible for coupling Dabbs with the word "bulldoze" on the Llano city to-do list.

Which is when Smith rediscovered it. The Texophile was out one night showing a friend historic buildings of Llano. Darkness fallen, a creaky swinging back door, creepy critters galore, and that overrun-with-weeds look made the place pure Hardy Boys Mystery as he recalls it.

Inspired, he made an inquiry into purchasing this "town embarrassment." Then-owner Rex Wooten informed Smith he would be a'dyin' any moment and Smith best quick get his rear in gear if he were to become the new owner. Of a small offer, necessary to make the deal go down, Smith says Mr. Wooten told him, "You have to do it tonight."

The rest is history, in more ways than one. Smith says the changing of the guard involved doubtful Austin friends unwilling to choke up financial aid ("You are a visionary fool," they said), one stoic and agrarian and tight-fisted farmer father bending his never-a-lender-be ways to pitchfork over a down payment, and seven years of elbow-greasing the place into its current condition.

Which, if you are expecting the Hyatt Reunion, then you best go on and book yourself at, well, the Hyatt Reunion. For the Dabbs Hotel, first established, as the sign says, in 1907, has hardly been updated. This is something those who like that sort of thing call charm and those who don't might politely refer to as a lack of basic amenities.

Two bathrooms serve the twelve rooms here. In winter heat comes courtesy of little clay-back gas space heaters. In summer, cool comes courtesy of little wall units. In each case, "little" is the operative word, and it is best to provide your own extra layers on cold nights and consider the finer points of nude slumber come July.

The one amenity you can get nowhere *but* the Dabbs, the real reason people make the drive through curvy swervy Hill Country and hang a right in the dirt, is this: Mr. Smith. For while you can know, to a degree, what you'll get (a small, brightly painted room, a creaky bed, and *My God! That Breakfast!*), you can never know just exactly what all Uncle Gary will surprise you with on any given visit.

He attributes who he is—a fascinating personification of an amalgamation of comedy, storytelling, culinary brilliance, feng shui philosophy, and a walking encyclopedia of Texas history—in great part to two people: his mama and *Old Yeller* author Fred Gibson, also a Mason resident.

Of his fairer parent he recalls, "She was a beautiful, flamboyant artist/entertainer," who exposed him to every medium. Of Mr. Gibson, he tells the fantastic tale of paying tribute—in elementary school, on stage—to the author, reporting on his books with the use of shadow boxes. Mr. Gibson, in the audience, congratulated the young Mr. Smith telling him, "It was the best storytelling of his books he'd ever heard."

So impacting was the author's encouragement, Mr. Smith says, "I harbored that in my heart forever." A storyteller, then, was born.

Now guests enjoy the fruits of those encouraging seeds. Sit on the front porch by the Llano piano. Or out back, down on the banks of the river in old metal porch chairs painted mint and lemon, cherry and chocolate, orange crème and blueberry vanilla. No matter where you plop down, sooner or later Mr. Smith is bound to wander by and offer up another story.

On a recent weeknight, just before a major holiday, the place deserted except for one party of three, the innkeeper has an especially good idea. The kids, ten and eleven, are still reeling with delight from a trip down to the old abandoned railroad bridge and a hike along the river throwing and skipping the smooth round white stones and the flat black stones embedded with nature's sparkling glitter. Everyone piles into Mr. Smith's 1950 Chrysler Windsor, newly awed, this time by the massive size of the automobile.

Smoother than a newborn's derriere, the ride through the crisp Texas night offers a stunning spectacle of countless stars, whiter and brighter than a toothpaste model's pearlies. Mr. Smith is driving his happily captive audience to the HooDoo Café in the nearby ghost town of Art, Texas, right on the road to Mason.

Alternating true tales of the Indians who originally lived in the area with how tiring it can be to be regularly whisked heavenward by the UFOS, the storyteller mesmerizes the kids who unabashedly pepper him with questions, begging for more more more.

After big burgers, fresh fries, and peach cobbler at the HooDoo, it's back in the Windsor and on to Mr. Smith's childhood hometown, Mason, where way up, upon the vista of Ft. Mason, he offers another history lesson. Gesturing at the little town's buildings and lights, he promises later a picture of the same area pre-European settlers. It's a promise he keeps the next day, digging out a favorite Texas history book, enchanting the kids once more.

Texas history drives him, he says. At the turn of the twentieth century, the rail line in front of the Dabbs Hotel was the end of the line. After that, travelers wanting to go further west had to take the Wells Fargo stagecoach across the frontier, through Indian territory.

When he took on reviving the hotel, Mr. Smith says, "I decided I was going to reopen the Texas frontier and invite the world to enjoy it."

That he has, regaling new guests with tales of past guests, who've traveled from around the world and the state to put in quiet time at the Dabbs: the musicians, actors, film crews, a famous opera singer, Bonnie and Clyde (yes, *the* Bonnie and Clyde), and once, even a Tibetan princess who surprised him by recognizing and delighting in Mr. Smith's pot of ham hocks.

They all know the secrets here: Manx cats sleeping on the back steps, mismatched sheets hanging out on the line to sun dry, the thankful absence of television, that soothing sound of the spillway nearby, the sunsets of rich red and orange fruits heaped into the bowl that is the dusky cobalt sky.

They sleep deep after a hard day's relaxing, dreaming of the famous No Checkout Time and those sizzle-hot skillets. Because at the Dabbs, there's got to be a morning after. And it's got to be as abundant as the day before, rich with the tales of Gary Smith, king of his own frontier. (2001)

## CZECH STOP

The aptly named Joy Powers sits back into the contour of a bright orange, hard plastic booth at Czech Stop, her place of employ for the last fourteen years. In a gravelly voice edged in the promise of a chuckle, the general manager says it's cliché-but-true: What she loves about her work is the people. Good thing, given the constant flow of customers who flock into the twenty-four-hour gas station/bakery/novelty shop/deli/candy factory on Interstate 35, at exit 353.

Owner Bill Polk opened the place eighteen years ago and hasn't locked the doors since. He simultaneously opened an adjacent liquor store, but when, as Joy explains, it became apparent that people weren't lining up for liquor like they were for baked goods, that space became the Little Czech Bakery. (It's still there.)

Describing Czech Stop to the uninitiated begins with a sort of "Who's on First?" exchange. First, you need to explain that it's West Comma Texas, not, as people usually hear, "West Texas," that vast expanse way over yonder to the left on a map. West Comma Texas, population just over twenty-five hundred, is roughly a hundred miles from Austin in one direction and the same distance from Dallas in the other. (Hence, the proclamation on the store's T-shirts: *If you made it here, you're halfway there.*)

The town of West bills itself dually as: "Czech Heritage Capital of Texas" and "Home of the official kolache of the Texas State Legislature." Kolaches (tasty little Czech pastries with fillings, often spelled *koláce*) are king at Czech Stop and the key to the store's legendary popularity among locals and travelers.

More than two million sail out the door annually. Thanksgiving Eve 2001 was a record-breaker, with eight hundred dozen sold in a single day.

Evelyn Cepak, the head of production, oversees the vast kitchen crowded with rolling racks of industrial baking trays, enormous stainless steel bowls exploding with warm, yeasty kolache dough, two mixers big enough together to put out 250 pounds of dough per batch, and an array of workers busy making the popular treats as well as countless other tasty items. (With seventy-four employees, Czech Stop is West's biggest employer.)

Ms. Cepak, on board for sixteen years, developed the secret recipe for kolaches using her mother-in-law's take on the traditional cake and refining it with another recipe she liked. She describes the distinctive flavor of kolache dough: "Salty sweet. It's not as dry as a cinnamon roll. It's not cake dough. It's not a bread. It's in between. It's egg-based. It's a soft product."

See, it's tricky. Your best bet is to plunk down some silver (most kolaches cost less than a buck) and let your taste buds mull it over. The variety of kolache choices can be daunting if you've never tried one, but fear not. The dough is the same for all of them, and the fillings are divided, more or less, into sweet or salty categories.

Along the lines of sweet, test: cherry, cherry cream cheese, strawberry, pineapple, blueberry cream cheese, poppy seed, cottage cheese, prune, apricot, and peach.

For those who love salt and eat meat, various combinations include pork and beef puffs, smoked sausage klobasniks, sausage and kraut puffs, and spicy-hot chubbies. Unlike their fruity counterparts, these pastries have their filling on the inside, not up top and visible.

Two big deli cases full of these doughy delights plus piles of freshly made sandwiches aren't the only things to feast your eyes upon. You could spend an hour or more perusing the décor and the "Stuff" ("Stuff" being the official term for all those things you didn't know you need that can be purchased mainly at convenience stores and gas stations).

The walls are lined with 8 x 10 black-and-white glossy photos of entertainers who have stopped at Czech Stop, no doubt on a road tour. Joy says this tradition started by accident when a band happened to leave behind a picture. Now, there are too many to count, and among the ranks are those who weren't famous when they first came through but are now. (These are outnumbered only by pictures of performers who weren't famous then and still aren't.) Among the former are Brave Combo, Southern Culture on the Skids, and Asleep at the Wheel.

And over here, just past the orange booths and right before the FONES (as the sign says), the flier for Red's Custom Hay Baling Service, and the Texas lottery-ticket machines, is a picture (on the left) of one Sparky Sparks. The grinning Sparky, sporting a straw cowboy hat and clutching an armadillo, has taken the time to scrawl, "Czech Stop's the only reason ole speedbump here is willing to get on the road. Thanks, Sparky."

Due east of Sparky is another classic: a picture of Jackie Bibby Snakeman. He has four rattlers hanging out of his mouth but strongly implies with his inscribed words that he would be willing to spit out those snakes in a heartbeat in favor of some Czech Stop goodies.

As for the Stuff, take your pick and come back often. The stock is ever-changing to reflect the times. These days, for a penny under twenty dollars, you can score a shellacked wooden wall clock featuring a collage including Old Glory, the World Trade Center towers, and Psalms 23. Or how about a fleecy sweatshirt emblazoned "God Bless America"?

And there will always be the standbys. Hillbilly luxuries such as back scratchers made from twigs and dried corncobs? Czech. Postcards of jackalopes? Czech. Wooden plaques featuring the "distressed" look and catchy slogans such as, "Grow Your Own Dope, Plant a Man"? Czech. Accouterments of alcoholism such as the extra-large Texas six-shooter shot glass? Czech!

Shelves burst with made-on-the-premises candy such as peanut brittle and rocky road. There are odd plastic toys, the kind kids' car-trip dreams are made of. Little straw hats embroidered "TEXAS" and made in Mexico. And not one, not two, but three West-originated books offering recipes and, in one case, history and memories of the town settled in the mid-1800s by the ancestors of many of those who still live here.

There's even a comforting sound to the place, a cacophony of small-town familiarity. In the distance, country music wafts from speakers.

Lead vocals come courtesy of the counter workers, such as Sherry, who on this chilly day also is teasing the UPS man for wearing shorts and sharing details of a friend's recent C-section.

In the *West Heritage Cookbook*, on a shelf in an aisle over by the hot deli, you'll find Agnes Marak's Kolache Recipe. At the end is a Czech proverb: *Bez prace nejsou koláce.* Translation: Without work there are no kolaches. (2001)


**BARNEY SMITH**

While some folks think the recent election results might best be placed in the toilet, Barney Smith believes otherwise. The seventy-nine-year-old San Antonio artist recently depicted an elephant and a donkey engaged in a tug-of-war *on* a toilet. There is no sarcasm or irreverence intended by his medium. Toilet seat art is Smith's passion and this is merely the latest addition to his growing collection, housed in his garage, a.k.a. Barney Smith's Toilet Seat Art Museum.

The idea for his unusual art form came thirty-two years ago when he stopped working. As Smith likes to say, "I'm a master plumber retired and I felt I ought to stick with my trade." The first seat featured dog tags—the K9, not military, variety. In the 572 seats since then, he's tackled many themes, painting, etching, and gluing items onto the lids, which come to him damaged but never used.

One seat honors the doomed space shuttle *Challenger* and includes a piece of the wreckage. Another bears barbed wire from Auschwitz. There are also seats with a piece of the Berlin Wall and ash from Mount Saint Helens. Many hold Indian artifacts and natural treasures: arrowheads, feathers, and birds' nests. Others display coins, license plates, trophy figures, celebrity portraits, and sundry bric-a-brac.

Excepting one, all pieces are lid-only. "I won't put anything in the hole," says Smith. "It's unbecoming. It looks too much like a toilet seat." (The one seat you can lift reveals a wasp hive beneath.)

For decades Smith practiced his craft behind closed doors. In 1992, a visiting artist came by to look at Smith's oil paintings. He was shown the toilet art as an aside. Excited, he alerted the media. The resultant attention convinced him to open his museum to the public.

It's an informal affair, open by appointment or when the garage doors are open. In addition to admiring the vast sea of seats filling nearly every inch of wall space, you can also watch an eleven-minute video montage of news clips touting Smith's work. There is no admission fee, and no, you can't purchase a seat. Only three have permanently left the building as gifts—one to TV personality Montel Williams, one to a toilet seat manufacturer, and one to Texan writer Bob Phillips. (Each of these has a replacement seat in the collection.)

Annually, around a thousand visitors from around the world sign the artist's guest book. "A man from Israel said, 'You did a real good job with the Star of David and the Hebrew alphabet,'" remembers Smith. The admirer later sent a postcard, which Smith framed. A few years later, he showed the card to another visitor. Turns out the sender was her husband.

When he isn't entertaining others with his craft, Smith and his wife enjoy traveling. His current favorite seat commemorates a trip the couple took to Switzerland last year for their sixty-first wedding anniversary. Hotel managers in Zurich and Wengen supplied him with treasures for his art. "We stayed in the Park Hotel in Wengen—owner gave me three sets of keys and a lock." In Zurich he also scored room keys.

The average seat takes twenty hours to transform into art. However, Smith says there's "No telling how many hours days and weeks" he spent on the one that has a cross, formed from sixty-two stones he cut and polished himself.

Paying homage to his religious beliefs is important to the artist. In the fifties he was a maintenance engineer for the Church of God Home for Children in Sevierville, Tennessee, where the children helped him collect arrowheads. "I had my preacher's license at the same time," he says. After seven years in Tennessee he was a pastor for a small church in New Orleans for a while. "Then I came to San Antonio and worked for Church of God in their printing plant. I was their shipping clerk, artist, and general maintenance man."

Smith promised his wife he'd quit at seat number five hundred, a pledge he has found impossible to keep. "I've been putting red on every exhibit number since five hundred because I've been in the doghouse since. I've been in the doghouse for seventy-two toilet seats."

Smith hopes to one day appear in the *Guinness Book of World Records*. He plans to keep at his work, "as long as the Lord will give me strength and I can stay out of the doghouse enough." His wife, he says, "thinks I've gone nuts here spending so much time on these things but I enjoy it. It's real relaxing for me. Good therapy for an old man."

To the best of his knowledge, Smith knows of no other living artist who shares his obsession with toilet seats. "There was a fellow in California—he had them hanging on the fence," he says. When that man died, his art was tossed.

Smith's daughter assures him that when he dies his work will receive better treatment. "They won't be going in the Dumpster. She may give them to some museum or something. She said they'll be intact. There are no toilet seats hanging in the Witte Museum [in San Antonio]. But some day there they may be." (2000)

## JOHN KARGER

John Karger is examining an injured Red-tailed Hawk just dropped off by a Texas game warden at Last Chance Forever, the Bird of

Prey Conservancy in San Antonio. Karger, the founder of LCF, extends a broad wing of the bird, and points to a broken bone protruding through feathers. The bird gives off a sour stench.

"Healthy birds should have a dusty, sweet smell," says Karger.

While assistant Kelly Rayner grips the hawk's legs to prevent any talon mishaps, Karger begins triage. Besides being a raptor expert, a master falconer, a bird behaviorist, and a conservation authority, he is also a veterinary technician. He gently tapes the wing, wraps the bird sandwichlike in a towel, covers its head to calm it, and sets it gently in a corner.

The next step is transport to Dr. Melissa Hill's veterinary clinic. Hill, president of the board of LCF, has worked with Karger for over twenty-five years to help rehabilitate and release injured and orphaned birds of prey back into the wild.

"By putting together his veterinary background and his falconry background, he can do a really good job with triage," says Hill. "Most birds are going to require immediate attention. If they sit around for three or four days, it destroys their chances. He's very good at initial diagnostics."

Karger's emergency treatment combined with Hill's quick follow-up increase survival odds. Nonetheless, Karger estimates this bird's survival chance at forty percent. Still, he says, "I'm not going to give up."

Behind the rambling ranch home that houses LCF, eight falcons and a large owl are tethered to perches. Occasionally they flap and hop. Mostly, they sit quietly, staring with otherworldly eyes, unperturbed by passing humans and Jesse and Maddie, Karger's father-daughter Jack Russell terriers.

While Karger has rehabilitated and released thousands of raptors back into the wild over the past decade, this backyard flock has permanent resident status. They are used for the four hundred educational programs LCF presents annually at schools, fairs, and clubs to improve knowledge of raptors.

Other permanent feathered residents—besides hawks, owls, and falcons there are Golden and Bald Eagles, an Andean condor, and vultures—are used for captive breeding and as surrogate parents or mentors to incoming birds. These mentors cannot be released due to physical or mental disabilities. But their teaching skills offer that opportunity to others.

On a gorgeous afternoon, Karger and three assistants set out with three Harris's Hawks. A twelve-year-old female and a four-year-old male, both nonreleasable, are working with a two-year-old releasable male.

"They have to know how to hunt and how to eat as a family," says Karger of the Harris's species.

The birds ride on thick leather gauntlets and are held by short leather tethers, called jesses. Once out in the field, they are let loose. They fly, perch on trees, then zoom in and perch atop long T-poles, constructed of PVC pipe, brought along for this purpose. Bits of beef heart lure them to the T-poles times they are reluctant to return.

Today's goal is to kill a rabbit. One darts out from the brush but finds safe cover again before the hawks can score. Karger switches to Plan B. An assistant extracts a thawed jackrabbit carcass from a thermal lunch bag, ties it to a rope, and runs through the field, dragging it behind. The hawks spot the rabbit and "kill" their prey.

The female moves in for the neck while the two males bicker over the midsection. Karger assists, using a pair of scissors to help divvy up the rabbit while he warns the birds to share. Once the two-year-old masters these skills—the average rehab takes eight to ten weeks—he'll be released.

Don Pylant, senior horticulturist at the San Antonio Botanical Gardens has witnessed LCF releases.

"We did one with Don Henley of the Eagles. It was pretty dynamic seeing him release an eagle. You're crying with joy, you're seeing a bird that once couldn't fly. And man, the one who usually does the damage to birds with guns or poison, in this case is responsible for giving the bird back his flight."

Karger says there is sometimes temptation to keep birds he knows should be released.

"I avoid temptation by not naming them. It's easier on the heart if they're not named," he says. He also feels a sense of elation each time knowing, "they're free and can do what they're supposed to."

Putting the birds' needs above his desire was a lesson that came early to Karger. At nine, he was given a group of baby barn owls.

"The first owl became imprinted on me. It fed my psyche tremendously. It seemed Merlinish. I was a boy wonder," he says. But the bird was hit by a truck and killed, which is when he discovered, "We're not supposed to raise them to imprint on humans."

A second owl also died. "I learned I was feeding them the wrong food—raw meat with no vitamins." The hard lessons gave way to eventual success. Three other owls survived and were released. Young John Karger had found his calling.

He gives his age as 5,005, offering and sly smile and palms crisscrossed with hundreds of lines as proof. Others dispute this, but not in an expected way.

"John is a living falconer from the sixteenth century," says Rick Johnson, putting Karger's age at a more reasonable five-hundred-something. Johnson, president of Talon Engineering in Arlington, has volunteered at LCF and sponsored the release of three hawks. "The art is in his blood. He lives for it," says Johnson.

Pylant agrees. He's watched Karger put on demonstrations for twenty years at the botanical gardens.

"He's the main draw," says Pylant. "We have several thousand people come. One year he couldn't make it. You never saw so many disappointed faces in your life. John is special. He helps people to touch nature and to let nature touch them. At every show there are tears, people are blown away."

After hunting with hawks, it's time to fly the falcons. Karger places a tiny leather hood on the head of a Lanner Falcon he's had for twelve years. The hood is a falconry tradition dating to the thirteenth century, when Emperor Frederick the Second learned falconry in Asia and introduced it to Europe. The hood covers the bird's eyes, calming it for the walk to the field.

There, Karger removes the hood and offers a series of commands to the falcon, which wears a radio transmitter to track him should he decide to circle out a little too far.

"Tail up," man says to bird. Bird soars. "Perch please," is a request for the bird to return. "Glove up," means "Get on the gauntlet."

"Duck on the pond," is the call to "dive for bait," and produces the most breathtaking results. Falcon dives, sixty MPH, wings whistling, pulling up mere inches from the ground. Karger rewards it with a dead chick, which the falcon clearly savors.

Looking at the bird, he offers a simple explanation, beyond

his calling to conserve nature, that feeds his deep connection to the raptors.

"I always wish I can fly," he says.                          (2000)


## WAX HAND

There's a hand in my refrigerator. It's orange.

If you were drunk and/or it was the middle of the night and you encountered it, this hand might startle you. You might think it was severed from a person who'd recently tested out some cheap self-tanning lotion on this hand. A person so distraught at the results that s/he immediately lopped said hand off and stuck it in the fridge for safekeeping.

To my surprise (chagrin?) my friends have yet to comment on this item. Maybe they expect nothing less from me. After all, I keep a spare stove in my bedroom and fake dog poo on the kitchen table. Or maybe no one has noticed it, hidden behind half-loaves of old bread, cartons of expired eggs, my ever-growing little-packs-of-condiments collection.

Regardless, from time to time, I spot it. And it amuses me. Takes me back to that wild weekend in San Antone.

As a writer, I am—like most in this odd subcategory—often forced to take on assignments-I'd-rather-not, if I wish to keep a steady supply of soon-to-expire food items in the fridge, and if I wish to accomplish this task via my writing.

For example, for two years running, I accepted the task of describing thousands of calendars. I can tell you anything you want to know about any breed of dog. I can also tell you about lighthouses, craggy mountain ranges, semi-clad women, and various European countries—other common choices for calendar photography.

Sometimes though, the rarest of rare, the most coveted of coveted assignment lands on my desk. TRAVEL GIG. I don't care if I'm being sent to California or South Jersey. A travel gig is cause to rejoice. Free hotels. Free food. Free tourist attractions. Expense account.

So it was with enormous pleasure that I accepted, without

hesitation, an invitation to travel a whopping one and a half hours from Austin to explore San Antonio. One years-ago trip to the Alamo and a couple of zoo trips notwithstanding, I'd never really checked out the place. Not snobbery. Time constraints and questionable car engines kept me from venturing down south for leisure purposes.

But now, waved before me was a proposition. If I could conquer and capture the wonders of San Antonio in fifteen hundred words, great would be my reward. Maid service. Food I couldn't afford on my typical budget. Plus that bonus writers love most: Money. I willed the old Toyota to go the distance. The old Toyota obliged.

With me: all-in-one companion/assistant/son—Henry. Hen serves multi-purposes. He asks more questions than I do. He's a handy excuse for me to show up at places suited to children without seeming conspicuous or perverted. We scrutinized lists of attractions suggested by friends, augmented research with shiny hotel lobby brochures, and planned our attack. By the time it was all over, fifty-four hours later, we'd averaged more than one stop per hour (not even counting time we slept).

As I sat to describe all we'd seen, I knew it couldn't be done. Fifteen hundred words is precious few when one feels compelled to include the expected (Alamo, River Walk, El Mercado, Tower of the Americas) and the unexpected (Barney Smith's Toilet Seat Art Museum, the O. Henry Museum). Too, there were the Buckhorn Saloon, the Cowboy Museum, Rosario's, Earl Abel's, the zoo, the Japanese Gardens, the missions, La Villita Assembly Hall, a state fair, the Institute of Texan Cultures, Schilo's, the Botanical Gardens, the King William District, Pioneer Mills, the Children's Museum, the library, the Witte Museum, "The Price of Freedom" at the Imax, and all those fun trolley rides. And more.

We fell in love with San Antonio and I said as much in my piece. Yet the first couple of drafts proved unacceptable to my editor. You see, this particular piece was for a custom publication. Custom publications are on-the-ground in-flight magazines, those rags financed in great part by the hotels where you find them. They are there to get tourists psyched. They can only offer happy, shiny articles that gloat about the destination in question. They must never suggest anything that might be perceived as negative.

Such as rain. Which I love. And which it did while we were there.

I recalled a glorious thunderstorm that drove tourists away from the Botanical Gardens. A storm which subsided quickly, leaving diamond droplets on the lush green foliage my son and I got to explore in near solitude. It was spell-binding. No matter. The rain had to be edited out.

As did the lightning—magnificent as we witnessed it on the horizon, riding the glass elevator to the top of the Tower of the Americas. Nix nix on that petrifying ride on the state fair Ferris wheel, too. (Too seasonal came the word from on high—never mind that it is an archetypal Texas adventure, to look down upon cotton candy stands and Mariachi bands and throngs of funnel-cake indulging, fat-assed, happy Texans shoveling it in.)

No rain. No lightning. No rickety rides. Then surely, surely, that hand would never make the final cut of the story. Hell, I didn't even try to work it in.

But that hand, which sits in my fridge, captures for me the entire whirlwind weekend, chastises me for all those years I sat, ignorant of San Antonio's bliss, bored on the porch in Austin.

We got it at the wax museum at Ripley's Believe It or Not. You go in. You look at the silly wax figures. You exit. Waiting to pounce on you are the minimum-wage workers, prepared to help you dip your hand in hot wax again and again, somehow managing to pull it off like a glove, color it, pack it in ice, send you on your way.

Expense account or not, our budget was dwindling. I nearly denied Henry this privilege, but the look on his face—that childhood eagerness—swayed me. We got the hand. We got the ice. But it was June, and a hot one, and the ice lasted about as long as a vegetarian in a corndog-eating contest.

We continued our exploration, but now a higher goal called. The bag with the hand in it dripped. The hand threatened to melt. We had to time our stops, track new ice sources at frequent intervals.

At Rosario's, the band blared, the food charmed our taste buds, and the hand sat, looking eerily real, silently warning, "Do not forget me. Ask for more ice. Or I will die!"

Mentally, I revisited horrible tales in the news, people rescuing actual hands and other appendages lopped off in horrid accidents. People who must find ice, right away. So this is what it must be like. Sort of.

The hand made it back to Austin. The summer just got hotter. Stubborn, I refused to turn on the a/c until well into July. One day, I noticed the hand starting to sag on the kitchen table.

I threw it in the fridge. Made vague plans to do something with it. But what? Take it out seasonally, like some peculiar Christmas ornament? Keep it in a bowl, daily renewed with ice? I never got around to any of this. So there it sits, fingers curled in fist of triumph, wrist twisted slightly—a reminder of that near meltdown, a secret well-protected hotel magazine readers will never have to know. (2001)

# EXPLORING ME, ME, ME

About a month ago, Rosie O'Donnell made new headlines. Not for telling the NRA to go to hell. Not for adopting her nineteenth child after accidentally sipping from Mia Farrow's water glass.

No. The latest from the Everything's Coming Up Rosie is this: she's taking over *McCall's* magazine, now *Rosie: The Magazine*. Her title: Editorial Director.

I could waste time wondering how the hell Ms. O'Donnell— who to the best of my knowledge has no journalism background— managed such a title when I myself, after seventeen years in the business, am still known to sometimes describe Chihuahua calendars to pay the bills.

But that would be catty. Spike would nevvvvver go that direction. Besides, Rosie's a star and we all know stars know everything, which is why folks like Rosie get to head up magazines and Suzanne Somers appears on the *New York Times* best-seller list.

Still, I've been thinking. I've seen *Multiple O's* or whatever Oprah's magazine tribute to herself is called. And then there's *Martha Stewart Monster* monthly, explaining how to knit martini coozies using only toothpicks and waxed dental floss. So what's to stop me from coming up with *Spike: The Magazine*?

Answer: *Absolutely nothing.*

Herewith, proposed departments for my monthly tribute to me, me, me, and those of you like me:

**You Suck for Beating Yourself Up All the Time:** A real look at the rampant self-esteem problem plaguing women everywhere. Each month, some nonexpert (probably me, maybe Suzanne Somers) counsels a "regular" woman about her need to constantly pick on herself for not being everything to everyone while never, ever weighing more than a 115 pounds. At the end of the interview, the expert/me would explain this woman sucks for beating herself up all the time. Before photographs would feature our makeover candidate crying tears of self-loathing. After photographs would feature her crying tears of joy for realizing she really is a worthy person after all *plus* she can still linger in the familiar territory of self-loathing because in fact, she does suck—for beating herself up all the time.

**Spinster's Corner:** Here I will monthly wax bitter, self-righteous, and holier than you towards lesser mortals who've found it necessary to pair off with partners. I will also endlessly dissect Neve Campbell and how utterly blind John Cusack is for falling for her when I was always out here, waiting. I will take potshots at others, like Mary Marcus, who wrote in a recent issue of *BUST* magazine, *"John Cusack Is the Man for Me,"* detailing why John Cusack is the man for her. When, in fact, we all know he is the man for *me* and I should've written that piece, damn it, and, since I didn't, he won't ever see it and dump Neve's ass and come running to me, hence leaving me in this ongoing state of spinsterhood. I'll also write a lot about cats, since I am acquiring them at a rapid rate, as all good spinsters do.

**Oh Really?** Based on an idea I had back in '94, when I traveled the country hunting down ex-lovers, hoping to videotape them answering my question, "Why'd you dump me?" I planned to edit myself into this documentary, responding to each guy's lame story, beginning my segments with, "Oh, really?" followed by what actually happened (since we all know I'm always right and those guys were telling big honking lies about what really went down). Unfortunately, none of the guys would answer on camera. (Though one, a sportsman whose southern-accented pronunciation of my name is "Spock," told me off-camera that he'd "thrown back a lot of keepers.") So this section might have to be fiction. Cool. Good magazines need fiction.

**Cathy Makeover:** We excerpt a Cathy cartoon—say, Cathy trying on a bathing suit, screaming "ACK!!" Then, I reenact the scene, only with self-esteem. For example, me sporting a thong and a Wonder-bra four sizes too small, nothing else, my belly hanging down to my crotch, that soft flappy stuff on the back of my arms jiggling. And I'd be standing there, grinning, two thumbs up, thought bubble reading, *"What a babe!"*

**Recipes for Disaster:** No women's mag is complete without a recipes department. Enough with food preparation already—if God wanted us to cook, She wouldn't have created takeout. No, these will be recipes for disasters, targeted at women who whine that their lives are boring. Tips like how to seduce the mailman, fun fake letters to "accidentally" leave lying where the kids will find them. ("Dear Honey, I know it will be hard for you to understand after thirty years of marriage, but I'm leaving you. Tomorrow.") Or, for the more faint of heart, good old-time pranks like how to put food coloring in the shampoo, or where to buy fake vomit to leave on the breakfast table.

**My Gol'dang Calves:** I'm tired of anorexic supermodels taunting the rest of us with their fat-free bodies. I'm tired of reading about women begging for advice on how to tone tummies, tighten butts, grow boobs. Let's celebrate our good parts. The best part of my body? My gol'dang calves. Solid as rocks from walking miles every day. Here, I publish pictures of readers' favorite body parts. And if it's a beauty mark on your right index finger, so be it.

**The Freakin' Car Rug:** My '85 Subaru wagon has one problem. The thing has, like, a Honda floor mat. It's the wrong size, bunches up under the clutch, pisses me off. Do I do anything about it? No. Unless you count mental notes to self to do something about it. But I don't. It just sits there, bunched up, pissing me off. Each month, readers send in stupid things they keep forgetting to do which would take about three seconds to do only they don't do it.

**Pack It On, Keep It On:** The fitness department. We list delicious, high-fat food favorites like fried potato salad, plus how much you need to eat how often to increase your weight by regular increments. Plus reasons it is better to have a ménage à trois with Ben and Jerry than it is to put up with your lame-ass boyfriend.

**Dump Him Dump Him Dump Him:** And finally, my advice column. I'm going to run the letters, filled with trauma and pain and misery, from women who want to know how they can fix their abusive, addicted, ugly-ass, dorky boyfriends and husbands. I won't say, "Get therapy." I'll just give the same advice every time: *Dump Him Dump Him Dump Him.* (2001)


## JOG BRA AVENGER

"Who's your alter-ego?" a friend asks me one night. (He, being a performance artist, has many.)

"The Jog Bra Avenger," I reply, unhesitant. I've never revealed this secret before. But then, no one's ever asked.

JBA's birth—if you tilt your head and wince at it just right (as my brother does when convincing himself the gas gauge does not read "E")—bears some semblance to that of Athena. Recall: Zeus swallowed Metis (don't ask), thus impregnating his head, from which eventually sprang his favorite goddess daughter.

In my case, the unwitting conception of JBA took place in '93, when my head was impregnated with some vague, noncommittal plan to lose a few of those very, very many pounds I'd conveniently forgotten to shed immediately post-childbirth, two years prior.

Initially, I felt stupid, walking daily four-mile circles to nowhere, lumbering along, my big slow butt blocking the path of the sleek, Lycra- and Spandex-clad joggers clambering to lap me, leave me to munch their dust. *What point, this folly?*

Leap ahead, a year or so. All pregnancy weight and then some is gone. Walking in circles makes such perfect sense now that missing a day causes great horror. Spandex and Lycra are no longer accessories to fashion crimes (as once I deemed them). Now I know the truth: these fabrics are gifts from goddesses, blessing me with comfort and--better still—control.

During the April-through-November Texas summer I can go for brisk walks, shirt-free, knowing my superhero uniform— O Blessed Jog Bra!—will keep my breasts from jiggling akimbo *and* allow me to work out in a state that is near-naked-yet-sort-of-tasteful. It is this confidence that prompts the Jog Bra Avenger to spring from my head, if not fully formed, then at least in pretty good shape.

She has been part of me now for nearly nine years. In cooler months, only I know she's in there, her uniform hidden beneath my T-shirt. Come summer, though, JBA is in full bloom, all over the neighborhood, bursting out vibrantly, highly visible, like the passionflowers she stops to admire along the way.

Thriving plants: these are the source of her strength. Each day begins the same. She passes the English garden with the roosters, proceeding south a spell. She is dragged along by those four-legged mutt sidekicks, Diablo and Sissy and Schmeckles, as they strain to run faster than speeding bicyclists, leap higher than stray Frisbees, stop gyrating sprinklers in a single bite, and so on.

They come to the dueling rosemary bushes near the house of the longhair calico cats. These are not just any rosemary bushes, but *the* perfect pair in the neighborhood. JBA discreetly runs a hand over them, pulls fingers to nose, inhales deeply. Her strength triples.

Onward now, past towering wild sunflowers, sunset pink blooms on spiky succulents, varieties known to her by their Catholic names: Rose of Sharon, St. Joseph's Coat, Wandering Jew. The tentacles of enormous century plants reach out, as if to wrap JBA in a friendly, prickly hello.

Others, too, all gorgeous, most with names that elude JBA, as if they are lovely, anonymous strangers in train stations, their mystery part of their allure. There are flowers she calls Barbie Bouquets, microscopic clusters seemingly waiting for the wedding day of America's favorite doll.

JBA scrutinizes all: pistils, stamens, petals, leaves. Her breath catches. She heaps shining-eyed approval and gratitude upon every one. Thus strengthened, she is now ready to focus on *the things out there that must be done!*

These things include, but are not limited to:

- Offering directions (real, true, and accurate directions!) to lost passers-by;
- Telling the time to the inquisitive and watchless;
- Offering moments of reverence over (while keeping the dogs from) corpses of car-annihilated squirrels;
- Promising to keep an eye out for Sadie, the lost border collie;
- Helping the frustrated blind woman gain special, top secret access the off-limits post office employees' restroom;

- Waving at small babies stuck in jogger strollers, saying, "Hey baby," and (whilst pointing at sidekicks) intoning informatively, *"Doggies!"*

JBA knows these things take extra time and can be challenging, especially on days when the heat rises like some transparent but insurmountable peak. But someone must be kind, must try to counteract society's pervasive and ever-growing rudeness.

JBA will do it!

Alas, as a close friend is fond of pointing out, there are many, obstacles standing firm between JBA and true superhero-dom. To be a real superhero, one must exert constant, steady patience. Truth be told, this is not the most outstanding virtue of either JBA or the one from whom she sprang.

JBA finds herself bad-vibing pedestrian-ignorant drivers who blab on cell phones, paying no mind to strolling avengers or children dashing through the neighborhood as if they were starring in the "What Not To Do" segment of some driver's education video.

Too, she has yet to stop herself from shooting dirty looks and certain fingers at leering workmen and catcalling perverts who "mistake" her up-top attire as come-on rather than for the support it actually is.

Then there are those at the Not-a-Drop-of-Scotch-Blood-Here public golf course along JBA's way. More than once—in fact, JBA sadly but honestly confesses that *many* more times than once—she has had a perfectly good superhero day ruined by a golf ball whizzing past her ear (and, once, hitting her hard in the derriere). At which point she is, naturally, forced to turn and yell, "FORE, EXPLETIVE EXPLETIVE!"

And, horrors, she has gone so far as to confront full groups of men holding silly little metal sticks, asking them *where the hell did they learn to golf anyway—Pep Boys?!* (All this while sidekick one shrinks in terror and sidekick two appears ready to leap into the arms of the puzzled men and nuzzle them to death.)

But JBA continues forth. She will not abandon her efforts. There are still fields of wildflowers in the neighborhood that need to be oohed and ahhed over (and the lot owners silently praised for not selling out to building contractors during the last boom).

There are beer-bellied men in tiny, Texas-flag running shorts that need to be stared into putting on shirts already (or at least jog bras).

And, on a brighter note, there are the glorious morning glories, which twist and wind up the trees and along the banks of a near-dry creek bed just over there.

These flowers hold a special place, remind JBA of her mother's garden back in South Jersey. They burst open each A.M. with inimitable bluish-purple cheer, trumpeting news from the home planet: *Okay, great, it's another day. Let's try to get it right this time!*

The morning glories, she has discovered recently, were made to be Eskimo kissed. Go ahead. Insert schnozz, inhale. That morning glory will wrap right around you.

This is the very best part of JBA's daily adventure, a reminder that if she keeps trying, it's going to just get better and better. Just look at how much better it already is, since she started those walks, over ten thousand miles ago. (2001)


## WARNINGS TO MY THIRTEEN-YEAR-OLD SELF

I went to a Bat Mitzvah on Saturday, my second one. The last one was nineteen years ago, when I was thirteen, as was my Mitzvah-ing friend then and my Mitzvah-ing friend this time.

I had no idea what a Bat Mitzvah was, what would happen, what it meant, or, for that matter, what being Jewish was about. I did notice that the party following the Synagogue Service sure resembled a Catholic wedding reception, and so, at its conclusion, I did what I'd learned from my people, the Catholics. I went up to the buffet, loaded up a few napkins full of little cakes, and stuffed my pockets.

Erica Schainbaum, if you're reading this: I'm *sorry!* I had no idea it was all you can eat on the premises, not all you can take home to your siblings, too.

This time, I watched my friend Janie, and remembered my own teen religious rite—Confirmation. Of how I stood, at fourteen, denounced Satan (Bad boy!), took an extra name, and let the funky-hatted Bishop rub a thumbful of Holy oil into my already pimply forehead.

**160**

Whatever lessons they taught me did not stick. Which is not to say I think ceremonies marking the passage to adulthood are wrong—I just think they should be different. I think there should be an official ritual for all thirteen-year-old girls, regardless of denomination. But make it realistic. Make it unforgettable. Gather the girls and shout a list of things to expect, a warning of the pitfalls ahead.

And what would be on this list? I can only go by my own experience. If I could go back in time now, with the painful gift of twenty-twenty hindsight, I would pull aside the thirteen-year-old me and I would tell me these things:

1. Stop feeling left out. You *will* get your period. And before you know it, it will stop being a mysterious wonder and start being a bunch of cramps and mood swings and scrounging for tampon money. And later, when it fails to arrive on schedule, it will be the source of agonizing insomnia and trips to the drugstore to spend your last twenty bucks on a pregnancy test. So, *relax* honey, and enjoy these last days of not having to think about whether or not you should wear those white jeans today.

2. When the boys snap your bra strap and comment on your budding breasts or lack of them, don't be flattered. Boys, very often, grow up into men who will continue to judge you first by the size of your mammary glands. And if and when you do get sick of it, and if and when you do confide in your French teacher and she tells you *your* behavior is provoking the boys, don't assume that just because she's older than you that she's smarter than you. She's not. She's just another reason women have been held back for so long.

3. When your mother tells you certain books and magazines are off-limits, to not dare read them—DON'T LISTEN TO HER. Sneak off to a library. Read smutty novels. Read feminist manifestos. Read Sylvia Plath. Read everything you can, the good, the bad, the truth, the lies. Then, I know this is hard, use your gut and decide what to listen to.

4. Learn everything you can about sex. If the teachers won't tell you, if your parents won't tell you, if the only one

who wants to tell you is a boy with a hard-on in a dark corner at the school dance, then ASK SOMEBODY WHO KNOWS. Go back to the library and get a copy of *Our Bodies, Ourselves*. Call Planned Parenthood.

5. Understand that, more than once, you will lose yourself totally in a crush. You will forget about homework and your girlfriends and any dreams you may have had of being strong and independent and you will only wonder one thing: How can I make *him* want me? Don't try to avoid these crushes—that's impossible. But promise yourself you won't try to change some part of you to make him love you. When he breaks your heart, start dreaming strong dreams again.

6. No matter what anyone tells you—like that high school counselor who says you should "just go to the state school and be a teacher because your parents can't afford to send you to a 'real' school"—remember this: you can do whatever you darn well please. You can go where you want and you can find a way to do what you want. And nurse and teacher and waitress and mother are all fine jobs, but only if that's what you really, really want.

7. There is a thing in this world called SELF-ESTEEM. It's about liking yourself and not feeling guilty about it. It's very helpful in the real world. At work. With boys. Later on with men. With parents. When daddy says you're stupid and some guy tells you you're not good enough, recognize that even daddies and boys you think are hot are capable of lying.

8. Touch yourself wherever you like. If it feels good, it's not bad, so don't tell the priest. It's not a sin. Don't bargain with God that you'll stop touching yourself if He'll answer your prayers. Pray for something else.

9. If your parents tell you you are their property until you're twenty-one, that you must listen and obey and follow their rules, nod politely. But keep in mind, you are free at eighteen. A legal adult. If they threaten you and say they won't pay for your school, won't let you walk out that door—just try to let them stop you. Pay for school yourself.

10. Remember it *is* easier when you get along with every-

one. Easier for *them*. But not everyone is worth getting along with.

11. Wait a while to have sex. It's like your period. You think everyone around you is getting it—you read it in the paper, you hear whispers of it in the hall. You feel left out. Don't. Because one day, you're going to wake up, and look at some body next to you, and think: *Ugh, now, THAT could've waited.*

12. When you are ready to have sex, use birth control. Don't hope for the best. Don't think you can handle a surprise pregnancy. And don't just give it to the first guy that comes along, I don't care how convincing he is. Make sure he's your friend. Make sure he talks to you. Make sure he *listens* to you. Make sure you talk about it, sitting up, with your clothes on, sober, in a well-lit place, BEFOREHAND. Then, if you do choose him, make sure you talk about it AFTERWARDS, too.

13. The first time you shave your legs, be sure to lube up first or it will hurt like hell the next day. Actually, it's a good idea to lube up every time.

14. Your best friend is not your best friend if she sleeps with your boyfriend, criticizes everything you do, and acts like she doesn't know you when "cooler" kids are around.

15. It is just as bad to give too much as it is to take too much. So forget about saving up two weeks' pay to buy a gift for some dork who a) is going to give you, at best, ugly earrings he bought for five dollars; or b) is going to forget to get you anything; or c) is going to not appreciate the gift. In fact, buy something for yourself instead.

16. You will encounter many people on the way. You will be overwhelmingly tempted to answer to the critical ones, to try to impress them, while you ignore the people who praise you. STOP. Listen to the supporters. Realize how much you mean to them. Mean that much to yourself.

17. Do not take the cordless phone in the shower so as to avoid missing *his* call.

18. You will have many chances to settle—for wrong men, bad jobs, foolish advice. Don't. Or, when you do, and when it hits you, stop settling. Get out. Try again.

19.   One summer, you will think it is a good idea to subsist solely on saltines and diet powdered ice tea. You will grow thin. People will compliment you. You will feel like crap. *Don't do that to yourself.*

20.   You will hit thirty years old. You will look back. You will think of all the things you wished you'd said when instead you stood by, quiet—so someone would like you. This is your final warning. *Say what you are thinking when you are thinking it.* You're probably right.

(1996)

## CAN I HELP YOU? *PLEASE?!*

Out driving at dusk one night I spot a small crowd. I pull over to investigate, stopping just short of hip-checking the others as I alpha my way to the focal point: one sprawled old man, pinned to sidewalk by gravity and age. His wife and I guide the ancient dude, still clutching garden tools, into his house.

This is not the first time I've aspired to be helpful without being asked. Nor, I confess, is it the first time I've semi-bullied my way into such helpfulness. Never mind Good Samaritans. My goal: better than good. And I will not stop until they give me that T-shirt I've been trying to earn for decades.

You know, the one that reads: *Best Samaritan.*

You recognize me and my ilk, an army of us marching toward you, overly helpful smiles on our faces, vast need to be needed in our hearts. We are *The People Who Volunteer Too Much.* And like it or not, we will assist you!

Mornings we leap from bed, eager: *Let there be a hunched over old lady who can't reach that can of peas! Give me a blind man to help across the street! If there is a fender bender slated for today, please let it be when I'm walking by, ready to render assistance with my cell phone!*

My quest began in kindergarten, when I took it upon myself to create custom-made condominiums from empty strawberry pints and fabric scraps for the newborn chicks we hatched in Mrs. Evans' class. From that point on, I have ceaselessly and diligently sought out good deeds in need of being done. At least by my perception.

Granted this occasionally backfires. So that *was* me who inadvertently kidnapped your dog. Brought him home. Called the number on his tag. Discovered, when you told me your address, I'd stolen him from your front lawn. Hey, maybe that'll teach you to hang a note around Barky's neck saying, "I live here. I'm just out for my morning whiz."

In which case, I'll just find some other way to be helpful. Like I did Thanksgiving of '88. Weighed down with the self-pity of being alone and a bellyful of Spaghettios eaten from the can (to dramatically underscore self-pity), I marched myself right on down to help the hungry.

Upon arriving at the Salvation Army I found myself surrounded by an army seeking salvation. Zillions of overenthused who, like me, seemed to think (if not admit) their presence among the Less Fortunate on a Joyous Occasion would net them frequent-flyer miles for future nonstop flights to heaven.

We stopped just short of fistfighting over who got to pour coffee for the poor. But I could not deny what my eyes and the volunteer coordinators told me. What they needed most for volunteers to do was this: Come back in the hell of July or some dull March day.

So I left. But I didn't stop volunteering. Over the years, with levels of success ranging from less than zero to satisfying enough to bring a tear to the eye, I have, among other duties, undertaken the following: blood donor, human milk processor, school haunted house coordinator, guest author in public schools, martial arts instructor, literacy teacher, eldercare giver, animal rescue newsletter editor, conference panelist, and fundraiser emcee.

Some gigs, like the literacy tutoring, were brief indeed. My student, an adult relearning to read after a brain injury, was too distracted by her family, the modern-day Munsters, to focus on the lessons. When her mother strolled through the house naked during my second visit, I knew I'd have to volunteer elsewhere.

Pasteurizing and homogenizing human mother's milk turned out to be a much better choice. Not only does this work help save the lives of critically ill babies, it also causes my friends to squirm like hell every time I bring up the topic. (No, the process doesn't really involve jiggling the moms and dunking them in hot tubs. Yes, I do sometimes claim that it does.)

Blood donation though, might be my overall favorite. I began Corpuscle Contribution in my late teens. While this bloodletting waxed and waned through my twenties and early thirties, lately I've been at it full-force.

Why the sudden resurgence in regularly having a needle the size of a chopstick shoved in my arm? Easy: they gave my one-gallon donor mug a couple of pints ago and ever since I have just been fixated on earning my two-gallon mug.

I don't even mind those five thousand embarrassing questions they ask every single time about whether or not you've had sex in the past twelve months with anyone who knows anyone who's ever thought about what it would be like to travel to a country where some guy lives who lived in England for more than six months back in the '70s while simultaneously shooting smack and having sex with fifteen anonymous male partners. I answer patiently. I must get my next mug.

When the World Trade Towers fell, a collective currency ran through the crowd that is all of us. *Here, let me do something now. Let me be of use, of help, of assistance.* Not an hour into the tragedy, blood banks were wrapped in ribbons of volunteer donors, lines snaking round buildings, down blocks.

Folks emptied wallets, pantries, closets. *Take this money, this food, these clothes.* New York was overwhelmed, not just with kindness but tangible goods: trucks packed so tight they did not include pallets, thus making the unloading that much more laborious.

Never mind the glitches. This kindness was amazing, wasn't it? How everyone stopped, if only for a few moments, to be extra kind, extra sensitive, not just to victims and their families but to strangers they came across in daily lives. A mammoth wave of volunteerism—formal and informal—blanketed America.

Which, okay, overall, was a very good thing. But damn if it didn't make it that much harder for us hardcore volunteers always on the lookout for selfless tasks to improve our sense of self. We've been left scrambling to fill our do-good quotients. Knocking other do-gooders out of the way, as I personally demonstrated, if that's what it takes to continue Volunteering Too Much.

I fear if the current pace of volunteerism continues, there will be far too little volunteer work for me. In which case, I'll need volunteers to step forward and demonstrate need, real or pretend. Just please, I beg you, let me help.                    (2001)

December 1, 1990. I am nine months pregnant, due on this very day. An earthquake is predicted in these earthquake-free parts. The first of two full moons that will make this a rare blue moon month tugs amniotic tide. Something big is coming.

Less than an hour left in the day, pain begins. I have been instructed to sleep when this occurs, rest for the journey. I cannot sleep. Cannot even sit still. Eager, panicked, I pace through the night. James, who can sleep, is conked out. Alone with my thoughts, I try to imagine things to come.

It is the home birth from hell. The midwife arrives the next morning. Lisa, my nurse friend, joins her. No drugs. No whale music, either. Just my howls bouncing off walls.

Fifteen hours into labor, the midwife panics. Maybe we should transport? We think about it. We think wrong. We stay home.

This baby is stuck, shoulders broader than my pelvis, a medical rarity known as shoulder dystocia, discovered too late to get to a hospital. Blind with agony and exhaustion I want to leave—room, house, planet. Let them finish without me.

They pin me down, back arched over beanbag chair, legs pushed over shoulders. Seventeen hours into it, words crash through the wall of pain otherwise blocking the others. *If you don't get this baby out on the next push, it's going to die.* This registers. I try to push. But brain has lost contact with muscles.

Houston, we have a problem.

Somehow the baby arrives. I can't see him though someone informs me I have a son. He is grunting, not breathing. Having aspirated amniotic fluid, he is drowning in the private ocean that kept him buoyant all these months.

This is not the movies. No one is congratulating anyone. James calls 911. Lisa sets up the oxygen tank. Midwife thumps tiny feet, shouts "Breathe, dammit. Breathe!"

I do not know if he is alive or dead.

The first paramedics are stunned. Home births are uncommon, they aren't sure what they're witnessing, cannot tell in the chaos this was planned. Unprepared, they call backup. Another ambulance. Door opens. Door shuts. Freezing blasts of air. Midwife screaming, "Shut the door, you're going to kill him!"

Passing cops spot ambulances out front, pop in uninvited. Miss Small Private Birth is now surrounded by an informal civil servants' ball, roomful of uniforms. I can't go with them. Vitals too unstable.

James goes on the long icy ride to the hospital where no one will pull over for the sirens. I stay home, midwife beside me, confessing this is her worst birth. "I don't think I can do this anymore," she says, wanting me to console her. Who will console me?

I do not get to meet him until the next day. He is in neonatal intensive care, a.k.a NICU. I am so beaten by birth that I am in a wheelchair. My left eye is scarlet red, blood vessels burst from the strain.

James teaches me how to wash my hands with solution, don scrubs. On the unit, I have no idea which baby is mine. James leads me through a maze of incubators. My baby. My God. Lying there, naked, tubes and needles everywhere, respirator down his throat. Someone—who?—says softly, "You can touch him."

I can?

This memory makes me cry. I spend my whole life trying to face off with full truths, whole big pictures. But this is one picture I have allowed myself to glimpse only fleetingly for a decade now. Him, looking at me when I turn to go, telepathing, "Why are you leaving me here alone?"

I leave him because they make me and I'm too tired to fight the imperative: Go home. Sleep. I'm afraid to disobey. I'm afraid they hate me for a home birth.

Covering his bases, the doctor says only, "He's not out of the woods." If my baby dies, he doesn't want the responsibility of false hope given. A nurse, angel on earth, does better. She pushes to get him off the respirator so I can nurse him. She shows me how to hold him so his tubes don't tangle. This is my unexpected picture of a newborn in my arms—needle in his forehead, taped hose across his face.

NICU is surreal. He is flanked by preemies born months before who do not weigh half his nearly ten pounds. I walk past other distraught parents. Not all of us will get to go home with full arms. I meet Paul, who has been left here by his mother to die. She can't bear to see him anymore. His belly is distended. His eyes search the room. He's been here a long time.

An open door reveals a room with several stiff little bodies. My stomach drops. Is this what they do with them? Double take. They are resuscitation dolls—you must learn CPR before you can leave NICU.

Another day I am in the pumping room, saving milk for my son who is finally improving. When I am finished, I learn the good news: he's off the respirator. James informs me he asked the child what we should call him the moment the hose came out. "Ennnnnn-rrrrreeeee."

*Henry?* I look up the meaning. *Ruler.* It's a strong name. We need strong. We go with it. I call my mother, tell her. Long pause. Then she tells me. This was the name of her brother, who died when he was a baby. I had no idea.

Through all this, I don't cry. Not until the day we drive him home.

Ten years is a milestone. Double digits for my little man. It's been a long, hard haul. I have learned, I joke, by my patented Error and Error system of parenting. I have made mistakes that leave me feeling nothing short of public flogging could serve due justice. There are things I won't ever forgive myself for.

But the one thing I got right is this: I never ever have taken this child for granted. I like to think that even if he'd had a perfect start this would be true. I believe that. But nearly losing him at birth, watching him watch me in that hospital, it all registered deep inside.

He is like the most elegant gift, wrapped in layer upon layer of brilliant paper. Each year a new layer peels off. Vocabulary and body grow. His feet are the same size as mine now. He scooters around the house, whizzing by me. *Watch me, Mom! Watch me!*

I watch. I watch the baby disappear and the young man arrive. Relish now moments soon enough I know I'll miss. Am daily renewed by a joy I could not begin to fathom that night the pains first came, as I wondered what might be.

I tell him one day, when he is grown, voice changed, we will go, both of us, around the house, looking for the kid who danced with the dogs and slept curled round the cats. It is bittersweet for me, glad that he can carry himself, sad I can no longer carry him.

We laugh all the time. I memorize that laughter, save it for when he goes away and only echoes of it are left to bounce off walls, the ways my screams did the day he came to me. (2000)


## LOVE HURTS BUT PAIN HURTS WORSE

We are all familiar with the professional euphemisms of "you'll feel a little push," and "some pressure," after which pain electrifies the skull . . .
—Paul West, *A Stroke of Genius: Illness and Self-Discovery*

I hold that there are three types of pain: purely mental; purely physical; and can't-tell-your-head-from-your-heart-from-your-ass combopain. I have suffered all three as have, I imagine, most of us.

The very worst pain I think I ever suffered came courtesy of the agonizing contractions of a late-night miscarriage which gave way to three full years of mental anguish, commemorated annually by my body cramping up on that very anniversary date until, finally, I gained the release that time does sometimes seem to bring.

These days, when I am hurting, I reflect upon those days. It's a warped therapy I learned from my mother who likes to tell her brood, when we are down, "to think about the worse-off." Like going out to the corner and observing a homeless, legless Vietnam Vet drunk and begging for Mad Dog change will somehow make me feel much, much better. Certainly it won't make me want to chain myself to this poor victim and then proceed to throw the both of us off the First Street bridge, will it, Ma? (*Oh no, dear, you'll feel much better!*)

Outside of this technique, however, are there other ways to remedy pain? Well, that depends. In matters of the heart or mind— when we are crushed by that human who two weeks ago was a mere stranger but by yesterday is suddenly "the one without whom I cannot go on living," or perhaps suffering what Holly Golightly termed "the mean reds"—it seems empathy is right around the corner.

As long as you know which corner to turn around, you can get someone to listen. In the middle of a nasty she-gets-the-house-you-get-the-Visa-bill divorce? Hey, so is that guy at the end of the bar. Guaranteed catharsis at the bargain price of whatever it costs to buy him another double Chivas.

Even if you are shy (perhaps yet another source of pain) and have trouble finding eager ears to hear you out, outlets for your psychological suffering abound. Every Christmas, for example, I fall into the funkiest of deep dark waters. Every year I try a new remedy. Most recently, I dragged my four-year-old away from his shiny, happy, sweatshop toys (*It could be worse, son. You could be earning five dollars a day to make Power Rangers in a poorly ventilated factory overseas*) at eleven in the morning on Jesus' birthday. I forced him, whining all the way to the movie theater, to attend the opening of *Little Women,* because I wanted to have a little breakdown, but I didn't want him to associate it with the holidays. Safe in the dark, I wept openly along with the rest of the crowd when the pouty Clare-Danes-as-wee-Beth ceremoniously kicked it.

When it comes to physical pain, though, it's been my experience that empathy of any variety is difficult to encounter. Even if you can get someone on the phone to listen, the odds of a personal visit longer than ten minutes are slimmer than Karen Carpenter.

My theory is that unless you are in corporal pain, you cannot feel it. If you can't feel it, you can't believe it is as great as she-in-pain claims it to be. "Get over it," is the message given when the agonized seeks comfort, even if that message is couched subtextually in the spoken, "You poor thing. That must hurt. Well, gotta go get my ferret dipped."

I understand this constant, overall lack of empathy for a couple of reasons. The first is the part of being a mom that insists I must dole out kisses and consolation and ice sponges and hugs every time he bumps into a table, cuts his finger, trips on the stairs, or sticks a hanger in an outlet. I go through the motions. I hold him and love on him. But I can't *feel* it. What I can feel is that somehow I must be a bad parent. Why? Because secretly I am wondering how many minutes until we pass beyond this episode and get on with our lives.

The second reason I understand uncaring sentiments is based on my own recent encounters with pain. In '94 I had four major (to my mind) episodes. These do not include the discomfort brought on by cold and flu—trouble spots that can be healed with juice and rest and a babysitter and a *People* magazine. These were events where I could, despite the agony and throbbing and bruised tenderness, sort of still move around. This, I feel certain, led my friends to believe it couldn't be so bad (i.e., *It could be worse. You could be in the hospital!*).

In February, I had a wisdom tooth pulled. Numbed to the gills, I knew nonetheless that if it took a strong man many, many hard tugs with a pair of pliers to complete the operation, surely it was bound to hurt later. It did. A lot. Blessed with a prescription for Vicodin, I pulled through stoned and groggy, baking Valentine cookies for everyone who lived nearby, calling the rest (some hadn't heard from me in years) to express my drug-induced dreamy love for them.

In March, what would turn out to be a benign freckle (a carefully cultivated beauty mark if you will) was deemed highly probably skin cancer by my dermatologist. Again, numbed, I lay on the table and watched (couldn't help it) as he sliced off the only thing Cindy Crawford and I ever had in common, as well as a nice chunk of my lower lip, and scraped it into a little jar. All this whilst pleasantly discussing upcoming plans for the weekend with his wife/assistant.

Though I could feel neither the slice nor the needle deftly tucked in then out, in then out, I sensed it would hurt soon enough. It did. Very much. There were no painkillers that time. And though the public could clearly see what appeared to be a number of fly legs poking out of my bulging lower lip, the most anyone could muster was a pained look. Definitely not empathy. Surely their own pain at having to view my face.

Things simmered down after that until December. Then a recurring ache recurred, this time relenting not. Another wisdom tooth. Another trip to the chair where it was decided much could be done to save the tooth, that there was space for it (thanks to some childhood molar removal pain years prior). All he had to do was get the damn thing to quit rubbing the tooth in front of it. This would require the aid of an "appliance." We set a date. He assured me the pain would be minimal.

When the big day arrived, my pain was so great, I didn't care if the appliance he had in mind was a washing machine. In fact, I was so looking forward to the procedure, I neglected to look down as I descended the steps of my son's daycare. First one and then the other foot flew out in front of me. Like a cartoon character, I sailed through the air, landing full-weight my hip against first a hard wood step and then the concrete. I sat, stunned.

Sensing (but not seeing—my eyes were slammed shut in agony) the tightening circle of toddlers gathering around me, amazed at my acrobatic skills, I knew the right thing to do would be to hop up and declare how little it hurt. I didn't. I couldn't. I could not move. A teacher's arms slipped around me, and she said in that teacherly voice, "You know, it's okay to cry."

So I cried. I cried and I cried and I cried. When I opened my eyes, they were greeted by thirty other pairs of eyes. The tears had had no effect. Not one child, least of all my son, gave any thought to consolation. They did not feel my pain. My pain, therefore, did not exist to them.

Someone suggested an ambulance. I grew defiant. Like one dazed in a car accident and looking for a distracting focus, I began to chant, "I must go to the dentist. I have to go to the dentist. I am going to the dentist."

I went to the damn dentist, all right. I told him of my new, far greater pain, literally, my pain in the ass. I suggested I might bite him if he wasn't careful. He looked at me the way Jeffrey Dahmer's guards must have regarded him, too, when he joked about using his teeth on their flesh. I quickly discerned that cannibals and dental patients do not evoke laughter for such punch lines, regardless of tone.

He numbed me to the point that I felt much like a Jack London character on an "I forgot the waterproof matches" day. He cranked open my mouth and placed a small metal rectangle, a single brace, an odd shaped staple, the iron lung of teeth—you decide—on top of the troubled tooth. The assistant stood by, sucking saliva with her dental Hoover. I sat filled with fear that I would swallow this $150 device and we would have to wait until I excreted it to begin again.

"Bite! Hard! Harder!! Haaaaarder!" he commanded. Though I

felt little, if any, pain, my growing expertise warned me that in a couple of hours the end result of cramming metal dental floss between two teeth to keep them from humping would top all prior pain. Correct, as usual, King Friday. In fact, it began on the drive home as the metal sliced the tongue that could not help but go back for more.

But wait, the good doctor had said little to no pain. Consequently, he has prescribed no painkillers. Sure, because I'd taken the last prescription sparingly—(my personal drug experiences have taught me that the character on *Mod Squad* who jumps out a skyscraper window after one half-hit of acid was based on someone just like me)—I've got a few back home. But soon the supply would be gone. I called and demanded more. The dentist responded no, there is no need, thus underscoring, yet again, my theory that unless you are in pain, you can't understand it. Also it pissed me off. What did he think I was, a junkie?

I called back, this time more threatening. Suddenly I recalled what a dental assistant said to me (why me?) the week prior: "I have to hurry to lunch. Heather has a one o'clock appointment and she's a pain in the butt." I wondered what they'd say before my next appointment. "Oh, Miss No-Tolerance has an 11:15. Let's pretend to accidentally mis-shoot the novocaine and needle around in there for awhile."

It took fully a month, but eventually the pain subsided. During my convalescence, I reflected greatly on pain and its occurrence in humans. I realized that when I am not in pain that suddenly crops up (a charley-horse, labor, a Dostoyevskian toothache, a stubbed toe, razor nick to the leg), I look for it. I have nine holes in my ear, one in my navel, and a tattoo that didn't exactly tickle in the application. People love to ask me how much these things hurt. How should I know? If they mean how much it hurt me to accomplish the feats, well, it hurt. A lot. If they mean, how much would it hurt them? What can I say? It won't hurt me a bit.

No matter how compassionate any of us are, we will never be more than spectators to another's physical pain. Helping someone through a rough spot is not really empathy. It might be martyrdom. Probably, more likely, a fear-induced attempt at good karma: a hope that you'll get soothing words and comforting strokes next time you get a knife stuck in your head. Other than that, it's all a squint.

I mean, I can describe for you my seventeen hours of labor and delivery, complete with details of a torn labia and all implied therein. I can tell you about the rusty nail I walked on twenty years ago. I even know, firsthand, what it's like to have gravel picked out of your face with a metal brush for four hours after skidding across a street on your cranial front.

Oh, I can make you wince, alright. But you'll never feel my pain. (1995)

# WHAT LOVE COMMANDS

Ghosts. His: abandoning mother. His last view of her, she's running from him and his siblings, one of them dead. He spends the rest of forever first in a foster home then shuffled elsewhere, wondering where she went, hating her for going.

Ghosts. Mine: controlling father armed with shame. Who tells me over and over how unworthy I am and why all I'll ever touch will fail.

Our ghosts collide in 1998. In each other we spot some mutual something which we mistake for in love though I now know was in pain. I am a mother the age his was when she left him, my son the age he was. My hair, like hers: long, brown straight.

Subconsciously I intuit—correctly, I quickly learn—he is the type who will be ashamed of me. This is my default landscape, though I keep swearing I will not return, not this time, not after the last one.

But here I am again, too good at this game to keep away. I know how to play. I tolerate it, embrace it, thrive on the idea that if I just try hard enough, keep up with the changing rules, dance the dance, sing the song, do it just right, *just the way he wants,* he will stop being ashamed. He will love me. I will win.

He expects: dedication, adoration, understanding, submissiveness. With rare exception he will not be seen in public with me. When we do go out, he will dictate the details. He will not invite me to company parties or to eat with his friends. He wants, upon demand and fully: my body, my time, my mind. I may not initiate. He will show up hours late or sometimes not at all because he forgot or fell asleep or an old lover really needed a shoulder to cry on. I may not use the word "girlfriend." We are not monogamous, understand?

Oh, and that dog has to stay outside.

He vacations without me, hooks up with a so-called ex. Comes home, confesses infidelity of flesh, weeps uncontrollably, begs understanding. I lunch platonic with a male friend, he pouts, protests, punishes.

When I say *This is wrong, I'm leaving,* he grovels, says I am the only warmth that ever touched the cold Antarctic of his soul. He says if I leave he might just have to kill himself. One more chance?

He packs for another trip. I watch. Did he leave that stack of condoms on the suitcase for me to see?

Again I storm away. Again he begs. Cries until he shakes. I cave in. Triumph is his once more.

Hypnotized, horrified at my own weakness, I cannot escape. Now and then, it calms down. Not good. This sort of nightmare needs drama to survive. So he casually drops into postcoital conversation comparisons to his other woman, lets "slip" terrible things she's called me, points out she's so much smarter than me. Smaller, too.

I get depressed. I lose weight. Lots of it. Now competing with a woman I don't know on a level so shallow it intensifies my shame.

One day, sad again (still) I call him. He won't answer. Emails me. *I'm here,* he writes. *But I won't talk to you.*

The game continues. He's the sadist. Guess who I am? I bite. I beg. *Pick up the phone please,* I write back. This drags on. I lose an entire afternoon of my life. I will never get it back. Worse, the burn of the shame remains forever.

I am worth so much more than this.

Some days I stay in bed, sick from how he makes me feel. He likes this. He can be the hero. *Poor thing. What's wrong? Good thing I'm here to help!*

Some something deep inside switches off. Out-of-body, I watch him crush down, heel jerking, grind my soul, cigarette into concrete.

Finale: I cut off my hair, put it in a box, give it to him. I no longer look like his mother. Still, it drags on a little longer. One night I call. He won't answer. I call again and again and again, shame now on fire. I cannot stop myself. I hate myself.

What has happened to the real me?

I go to his house. I do something I have not ever done before. I jump up and down on the lawn. *I gave you everything I had!* I scream. *You gave me anger,* he taunts back.

He takes no credit for this anger of mine—him with his ever-changing rules, avoidance, philandering. Of course I'm angry. And he hates this anger. Because it is the part of me he cannot control. Because it is the burst of fuel I need to finally get away.

A week passes, maybe two. I call, broken, sick, depressed, desperate for closure. He refuses to talk.

A year passes and then two. I improve. I like myself okay. I work on being centered. This involves not dating. Just as I know I cannot trust myself to stop at one drink, I sadly acknowledge that I cannot recognize a controlling man. Or, worse, I can, and I find this irresistible.

Then one day, at school, I spot him, though he is not a parent. He has found another. A mother with a child at my child's school. This new woman, too, has his mother's long straight brown hair.

I think Son of Sam.

I look past him. Hold my head up. The urge to double over and puke is real though. I am Alex in *A Clockwork Orange*. He is Beethoven's Ninth personified.

As I do with problems now, I meditate on this resurfaced ghost, seek peace from the daily haunting. I breathe deep, focus, try to target the specific pain point as a first step in eliminating it.

Against my will, lip trembles, hot tears bisecting cheeks. One word flashes neon in my mind.

*Shame.*

This is the problem. *Shame.* What I feel whenever he passes me now. Whenever *they* pass me. They live nearby. There are so many bicycle routes in the neighborhood. They choose my street as their normal course.

I wonder if he shames her, too. If so, what will her daughter take from watching her mother shamed? Will she grow up to seek it, too?

I wonder what my own son thought, watching me, sick with shame. I pray he remembers only that I fled. That he must always do the same. That he must never use shame to control.

I fight the irony of self-inflicted shame as I acknowledge the role I played, letting him shame me. Lying before him like a welcome mat: Wipe your filth on me.

*You idiot,* I say to me, remembering this.

I contemplate the words of novelist Haruki Murakami:

Results aside, the ability to have complete faith in another human being is one of the finest qualities a person can possess.

I am not an idiot. I gave true love in complete faith. There is no shame in that.                                          (2001)

## CRUSH

### I

Bob and John and I are at a hoot night at The Red Eyed Fly downtown. Hoots are live tributes to nationally famous bands (cult, pop, rock) by local obscure bands (various genres).

So, at the Prince hoot night, for instance, an all-girl group, a sensitive singer-songwriter, a ska band, a punk outfit, a sugar-pop rock ensemble, and others offer sundry renderings (serious, campy) of "I Would Die 4 U," "Nothing Compares 2U," "Little Red Corvette," "When Doves Cry . . ." U get the picture.

On this hoot night, the honorees are Guided By Voices. I don't know the band's music. Likewise, I don't know Bob. He's just here, along for the ride with John, my dedicated friend going well on two decades now. They're doctoral candidates, it's spring break, and Texas is a sight warmer than Lincoln, Nebraska—where they pay their rent. I'm queen of sure-come-on-down, eager to share my weather, my porch, my penchant to feed all.

So here we are. At the Fly killing a couple of birds at once. I'm showing off what my adopted hometown, Austin, claims to be most famous for (self-appointed title: Live Music Capital of the World). Also, I'm here to see and show off Ricky.

Ricky is the drummer for the Druggists. He is my latest crush. The night Bob and John arrive at my house after a dozen hours of driving, they interrupt what is maybe going to be the beginning of a torrid sex affair between Ricky and me.

I say maybe because when push comes to shove—the culmination of months of flirting with this drummer/grocery stock boy many years my junior has him sitting on my bed's edge, me strewn beside him—Ricky suddenly gets nervous as a fourteen-year-old. Neither one of us knows where to begin. He tries verbally lubing things up by asking what my bra looks like, a question that makes me want to laugh in his face. A reaction I suppress but, in being aware of it nonetheless, I sort of begin to face the fact that this proposition is utterly preposterous.

Still. Though my faith in Ricky is fast waning, though I'm beginning to understand now that all those long nights of pontificating were not really moments of brilliance (as I, in my crush-tinted glasses made them out to be) but rather the rantings of another barely-employed Austin musician/pothead—despite all this—I have sort of bragged to John and Bob about Ricky. Because I can be ferociously foolish and dedicated that way, touting far too loudly attributes that I realize only later hardly exist, if they exist at all.

This is not entirely Ricky's fault, this inexplicable crush of mine on a man with whom I have nothing in common. Nor is it entirely mine. This thing that has materialized between us is a combination of my worst pattern and his basic survival skills.

My track record for awful-mate-choices precedes me. So great have been my errors, I once published a book on the topic. Things haven't gotten better. Now I suffer an added burden—unsated while sexually peaking—having recently crossed the threshold of thirty-five. Thus I find myself doing things I wish I wouldn't, like going to movies I know will be awful just to catch a glimpse of some young male actor (Mark Wahlberg, Heath Ledger) sans shirt. So I can dream a little dream, if only for eighty-nine minutes at a time.

Ricky suits me because he's got some weird, masculine Mae West lexicon combined with a "Pleased to meet you Mrs. Robinson" sheepishness going on. For example, Ricky is fond of "accidentally" letting slip that he's got an enormous cock and an even bigger desire to put it somewhere and do I have any suggestions for him? We both know (but pretend not to) that he's stringing me along in a manner that will net him food, comfort, adoration, a ten or twenty spot here or there. For my part, I receive the sort of false flattery that I am a little too fond of anymore.

The Druggists take the stage. It's an outdoor affair. Rain spits. A surprise chill in the air. A tent offers some shelter but Bob and I opt to stand beyond it, on the edge of all. John has wandered off. Bob is talking about music, how rock is okay but it's jazz and classical that take him to places so blissful he can hardly describe them.

I am aware, peripherally, of Ricky bashing on his drums. I am aware, too, that my job as she-with-crush-on-Ricky is to be drinking in his every move.

But Bob is pulling me in. I'm pretty sure he's not trying—this doesn't feel like flirt. But infectious passion spills from him, wraps around me. How can one feel this deeply about anything at all? I want to feel this way. I listen up.

Bob says that, should the universe ever decide to strip him of one of his senses, he prays it won't be hearing, life without music being too painful to contemplate. (Ricky bangs harder now, mouths the words though he is not miked, makes rock star hand gestures and head bobs. The lyrics: *I believe you, no need for further questioning . . .* Ricky, I have to say, looks pretty stupid.)

There's something odd about Bob. What he's saying and how he's describing it—were he anyone else—most likely would land him, I believe, square in that conversational place bounded by these clear parameters: pompous, arrogant, pathetical, posed.

But sincerity is a true thing, one you can grasp with all your senses if the person emanating sincerity is, well, genuinely sincere. Which Bob clearly is. He is not lecturing, proselytizing, or showing off as he speaks of what moves him, launching into a moving recitation of "On Angels" by Czeslaw Milosz.

I listen, as closely as I can (the Druggists are really kicking into it now) and discern that, oh glorious synchronicity, while Ricky wails on the skins to Guided By Voices, Bob offers up thoughts on being guided by voices.

> The voice—no doubt it is a valid proof,
> as it can belong only to radiant creatures,
> weightless and winged (after all, why not?),
> girdled with the lightning.

His love of audibility thus illustrated, Bob segues gracefully into how he believes one day he might just find his true love and know her immediately by the sound of her voice (self-conscious thoughts of my own voice register: loud, harsh, Jersey-accented).

Wetness—Tear? Cold raindrop?—shines on Bob's cheek as he speaks. Something is exchanged telepathically between us. This is the turning point. I look at Ricky up on the stage. At that moment, it occurs to me: *Rock and roll is fear of intimacy amplified.*

After the show, Ricky is nowhere to be found. I know he knows we're here. But he has made no effort to stick around, find us. John, my friend through so many crushes, senses my unspoken discomfort, knows I'm already spinning false it's-no-big-deal excuses in my head. He rescues me, announces the rudeness of Ricky's behavior.

Back at the house, little open-flame gas heater on the wall poor imitation for the roaring fireplace I wish I had, I sit and listen to Bob. He takes me places I forgot existed. Other places I do not know. We are talking poetry and philosophy, passion and what he calls his "little pool of pain," the result of a recent divorce, palpable to me across the room.

I wake up the next morning, changed. Doesn't that sound dramatic? Is it how these things work? Black. White. Loyalty applied. Loyalty withdrawn. Allegiance transferred in a heartbeat. Some unplanned, sudden and irregular beat of the heart transferring allegiance for me. Without consultation. I have no say in these things. They just . . . happen.

A vague film of Ricky-crush continues to coat me, the residue something I must scrape off each time I encounter him over the ensuing months. But the spell is broken. I have seen and heard and felt something else. Something much better than Ricky.

Its name: Bob.

Thus, like that imperative on the side of the shampoo bottle (Rinse. Repeat.), again it begins. Crush anew. Goodbye Ricky. Hello Bob. Welcome to the wacky world of my mind where, if you (*you, new object of my desire*) were conscious of it, if I could somehow influence your dreams, you'd wake in the night to find yourself the protagonist of more than one bizarre fantasy of mine.

Yes, suddenly you, whom a week ago I did not know, are the star. Now that you are discovered, I can't see how I ever thought of even thinking about casting someone else.

It spins. Out of control. Stomach flips. And then. Grinding halt. We will not. Do this. Again. NO!

God I am sick of it. *Crush.* As a verb certainly it is nothing if not violent. We *crush* bugs. Men who could walk yesterday are rendered paraplegics today because they got *crushed* by heavy machinery. The only possibly innocuous definition of *Crush* pertains to a sickeningly sweet, artificially flavored soft drink. And even that rots the teeth and fills one with empty calories, costs far more than it's worth, certainly cannot be mistaken for anything healthy.

So there—an informal etymology of the word for the condition I have succumbed to ceaselessly. *Crush.*

I fucking hate it.

## II

Kindergarten. Clear memories right down to what I am wearing the first day. Blue dress dotted with colorful little houses, topped with a big white collar, centered with an orange-red tie, this outfit sewn lovingly by my mother. Red patent leather Mary Janes. Paper turtle nametag.

Teacher: Mrs. Evans. First crush: John Logan. One day I ask my mother *Can I please bake him a birthday cake?* My mother, deeming this too extravagant, and possibly influenced by her own girls-don't-pursue-boys upbringing, applies kabosh to my simple dreams. I don't ever forget.

In second grade, I decide John's brother, Dave, is cuter. Transference.

I write Dave a note. A really nice note. On my good stationery, the stuff printed with neon-colored zoo animals. I do not consult my sage mother. So I have no one but myself to blame when it is returned, shoved in the mailbox, scrawled over in obscenities.

Some sort of permanent message registers. It's taken me years to boil it down. I've gone over it for hours, weeks, months, years, and now decades. Boil it down. *I just want to connect.*

Dave Logan does not.

After John and Dave comes Jimmy Monsu whose hair-pulling and skin-scratching my mother informs me is borne of desire for me. Then Jimmy Richardson appears (for whom I take a nail in the lip as I—attempting to time an Evil Knievel jump on my Schwinn up over the uneven driveway curb to coincide with Jimmy's biking by on his way to midget football practice—hurtle off of my wheels and onto the ground, face connecting with nail, just waiting there to crucify me with embarrassment).

How many of them there have been all these years. And how I've fixated on them all. I never stalk. Tres gauche! As Jimmy Carter lusted in his heart, so I silently follow those I fancy in my imagination, inventing where they are and what they are doing and with whom. I am searching, searching in my mind for that weird specific something that flips the switch that casts the light on the notion (strange, I know): *There he is, the one, with the solution, to it all.*

And so, many years and crushes later, as Bob postulates finding *her* just by *her voice*, so I conclude (oh at last!) that one certain characteristic always identifies *him* (whoever he is at the moment). The characteristic, simple: *unavailable.* In a variety of flavors: disinterested, evasive, married, gay, lives thousands of miles away, etc.

Identifying this thing, this unavailability, provokes a sensation like that evoked as beer bottle cap twists until, pffffft, the exact moment the air escapes and with it, some unspoken promise in the release. Here is the promise: *Stick with this, keep at it, and you will be rewarded.*

The promise, of course, is false or temporary at best. Yes, drink the beer. (Indulge the crush fantasy.) Escape for a while. (Get giddy perseverating the details of your crush's perfect characteristics.) Drink more. (Overindulge the fantasy until you are paralyzed.) Dance naked on the bar. (Envision the life together, the wedding, the children, the JOY!) Find yourself puking, hot wet beer puke. (Cry hot wet tears of heartbreak when crush manifests not as true love after all.)

*Crush.* (Don't tell me you've never had one.)

Fifth-grade-heart. That's when it stops maturing. Fifth grade. I don't care where you get your hair done or how big your suv is or how fat your portfolio or confident your bullshit façade. You run into *that person* who makes you, almost beyond will, want to do anything *anything*—abandon job; abandon spouse; conduct self as complete fool; dress inappropriately; fellate (though, ahem, that's *not* typically something you're fond of) to possess that person, and there you go, fifth-grade-heart takeover. No escape.

With Bob, as with them all, I come up with lists of great reasons why this crush is actually much better, more acceptable, and healthier than the one immediately preceding it.

In the case of Ricky, the excuse for selecting him is that I'm not getting bogged down with deep cerebral connectivity. Picking Ricky is acknowledging that life as I know it is swell, thank you, I don't need some "other half" to complete me. All I really need is a little bit of getting it on to ice my cake.

Thus Ricky is (I tell me) better than the one before him, because I was too willing to invest too much in whatever it took to gain some permanent something with *that one,* which—once Ricky arrives to make me see things differently—I *thought* was a good idea but now I see how self-defeating and time-sucking it would have been to get tangled up like that.

With the introduction of Bob, all Ricky rationale sails right out the window. Sequential crushes, I've found, have a way of canceling each other out. What Bob does to my brain—makes it feel bigger, smarter, embraced—negates what suddenly becomes the shallowness of the now disdainful Ricky. (Yes, the very shallowness I once convinced myself was so buoyant! So refreshing!)

As Ricky had a list of priceless attributes (young, cute, horny, music lover) Bob gets one, too: He's so sensitive! He's so smart! He doesn't tease me! His writing is so intense, like messages from some home planet! He adores his ex-wife (imagine!). He's kind. He can walk on his hands. He understands I'm so sensitive! He *understands!*

### III

Ross is my best friend. He's gay. He knows all about crushes. Mine and his. He can simultaneously roll his eyes, giggle at my poor skills in selecting decent straight men, and hold my fifth-grade-heart in both of his big warm hands, like it's a freshly hatched chick needing nourishment from an eyedropper.

I joke about how—us both rapping upon the door of forty, both still "available," both swept away by the youth and beauty of the very same unknown young men we walk past on the street (the ones who do not return our stares)—I joke about how this is our *Death in Venice* stage. Usually we laugh at my joke, but some days I panic, humor of the sentiment sucked away. I think: *Oh god this really is it. I am alone. And that's how it will be. Forever.*

Other days—Is this a gift of age? Of having spent more adult years single than not?—I put the fear under the microscope.

*What is it I'm so worried about?*

Answers:

- I will never be wholly and completely loved by just one other.
- I will never have good in-love sex again.
- I will become increasingly crabby and reclusive.

- I will become jaded and not even realize it and what a bitter old lady I'll be when I could've found joy through another.
- My hope that, no really, there is someone out there, someone who connects completely, is one hundred percent bullshit.
- I am a jackass for having hoped.
- Me: Jackass!!

(Did you see that? More boiling down.)

Now, I apply the lens of logic to the microscope, refocus, look again. *Think about it,* I tell me. A new list materializes:

- I had a child with a man I loved with all of my heart, a man who left us not for lack of love but because grave illness stole him away.
- I am hardly alone in this world.
- Besides this child, who is the most amazing human I have ever encountered, I have no less than, literally, dozens of friends.
- Among whom are no less than many many men, all of them beyond decent, kind, loving.
- The women, too, are nothing to sneeze at.
- Collectively, they all love me and I love them.
- I am so blessed to have such a full life.
- Me: Blessed!

Ross again. Let's face it: I am in love with a gay man. This is no crush. This is serious. There is *the connection.* Always. Wherever I am—if I am laughing my head off, if I am bursting out crying—he is the one I want to call. If I am scared, he is the one who calms me. In yoga, we do an exercise. *Breathe deep, picture in your mind's eye someone you completely revere.* Ross's face floats into view every time, filling in the dark places.

The other night, I'm mopping the floor. My crush on Bob has receded—remnants still come to me, dance through my head, but the painful when-will-we-next-talk anxiety is gone. And all I can think is, *Wow, mopping the floor is SO much more fun than having a crush.*

I have a little notebook. It is full of written odds and ends— a diagram of a Tarot card reading that confirmed what I already knew (my last lover was a cheating son of a bitch). A list of books I've read. A list I'd like to read. Phone numbers in absolutely no order, many belonging to people I no longer wish to converse with (in particular the cheating son of a bitch).

Among this inky flotsam and jetsam is a mini set of notes. I remember where I was when I wrote them. At a bar. Listening to Paul play sax. In the bar, while he plays, dramatically I note the similarity between my feelings for Paul and the feelings exhibited by the main character in the French movie *Therese,* a rendering of the life of little St. Theresa of Lisieux, who begged and begged to be allowed in the convent at a very early age. This is because, as portrayed in the film, she has what can only be described as a crush on Jesus. It's been years since I saw that film and still I hear the nuns giggling, giddy, knowing they are the brides of Christ! Christ! *Isn't he so cute?!!*

Unlike Ricky, Paul never makes it to the regret column. Time just passes. The friendship goes on. My crush feelings remain a secret (or else Paul just politely feigns ignorance, waits for me to work my way through). Then these feelings, they go away.

Sometimes, it happens like this—one crush dissipates before the next one forms. In these rare instances, I suffer a disturbing calm. I wake up in the morning, wrack brain to focus in on who it is we're fixated on these days. Brain comes up blank. Leading to all sorts of healthy, calm, hopelessly dull behavior. Things get accomplished.

Is this why I keep finding them? Crush after crush. *Crush crush crush.* Crush the peace. Crush the solitude. Crush the tentative acceptance of single life as enjoyable possibility. What is life without drama? Crush is perfect drama. One-sided, in the head, the crush himself unaware and so unable to sully the crush by, well, crushing it with a declaration of disinterest. As long as a crush remains a crush, a crush offers hope. False hope = Better than no hope.

Wait, that's right, isn't it?

In the trunk of his car Bob carries a bullwhip and an 8 x 10 glossy head shot of his ex-wife. I find these things more appealing than I can capture. How absurd: bullwhip and ex-wife. How odd, what he does with these things: holds her up, declares her flaw-lessness with a pained catch in his voice (the pain resonates, in-creases his attractiveness: *He needs to be taken care of! I can love him AND be useful!*). He cracks the whip.

During Bob's brief visit, my neighbor's rooster escapes. We go to wrangle the rooster back into the yard, behind the gate. It is a shared experience. We are conspiratorial. How does one motivate a rooster? Hahahahaha. *We have no idea.* We are so silly as we try. This is funny. A together moment to remember!

Who wouldn't have a crush on him?

The crush is like arthritis or asthma. You can't know when it will flare up. It's chronic. It affects the ability to breathe, to move comfortably. It aches.

It also causes a bizarre associative disorder, which I shall hereby officially dub Red Toyota Pickup Syndrome (RTPS). This syndrome dates back to Tony, whom first I boinked, second I attempted to get to know, third I found myself abandoned by, and fourth, I then developed a crush upon. Tony drove a beat up old red Toyota pickup truck. He drove it right out of town, moving far away not too long after we met.

To this day, I still see an absurd number of red Toyota trucks, though I swear to you that prior to my crush, Toyota made not red trucks. Likewise, when Ricky was the focus, I could not listen to music without the drums completely dominating.

With Bob, I have, perhaps, the strangest bout of RTPS to date. Out for a walk, I spot, a block or so away, a woman with a dog. She appears to be rocking back and forth convulsively.

I move closer, increase my pace, until I am running, cell phone unsheathed, ready to pound out 911. I see, as I approach, that this is a seeing-eye dog, harnessed. The woman is blind. I offer my assistance. Acting as if I, too, must not be able to see, she gives no explanation for the wild thrashing about I have witnessed, merely explaining she is lost.

In fact, she isn't. She names the street she seeks. She is stand-ing at the corner of it, inches from the sign saying so. The sign she cannot see. I help her. She's gone.

As I walk away, my mind digs through the files, pulls up the one with Bob data, relates this incident to his speech in the cold rain about how if a sense left him, please let it not be his hearing.

Are you laughing at me? I confess that I am laughing at myself. How amazing, this crush-addled mind of mine, to be able to find hints of Bob everywhere, even in the convulsions of a blind stranger, trying to find herself when she isn't even lost.

If there is any "good" thing to come of this—the ongoing agony of the unbaked cake, the hair pulled, the obscenity covered love note, the nail through the chin—it's that even I am learning, maybe thirty years too late, that *crush* is not precisely the same as *kill*.

Come to think of it, I have lived through them all.

I call Bob the other day. He asks how I'm doing and I confess my latest farce. I am listening to the radio show of a man I've met at a party, a guy I think is pretty nice. I've been mulling whether he is crush-worthy. At first, seeming maybe even mutually interested, I deem him not unavailable enough. Now, though, he has dropped out of sight, and, contact cut, left me nothing but time to erect a pedestal beneath his absent feet, the task I am now busy at.

Bob wants to know if the radio show is good and I say I'm not sure. I'm so embarrassed at my own behavior that I have it on in the other room. As if, should I enter the same room as the radio, this pending new crush might look straight through the receiver, see me listening to him, mock my hope.

I'm not ready for that sort of thing, real or imagined.

Then, decrying my own goofiness, I whine to my penultimate crush about my newly forming one. "I was in *that place*. I was *happy*. That brief moment where it was just me and my books and the kid and my mop. Peace! No troubling crush. And now, now here I go again. God it takes so little to get me going!"

I pause.

"Really, would you have it any other way?" Bob asks, soft, in that thoughtful calming voice of his, as if he's just found me thrashing about beneath a sign I cannot see. A sign revealing I am, after all, just where I want to be.                                         (2001)